FIELD OF GRASSHOPPERS

by
KEN DAHL

Copyright © 2014 Ken Dahl
All rights reserved.

ISBN: 149547528X
ISBN 13: 9781495475283

This book is dedicated to my four sons,
of whom I am extremely proud.
My children (and their wives) have become my teachers.
I didn't see that coming.

Acknowledgements

First and foremost, I would like to express my gratitude and joy for the luxury of my very supportive wife, Liz, who has not only encouraged me and inspired me throughout this entire project, but has become somewhat of a "pastor" to me concerning my spiritual growth. I'm sending a huge thank you out to the countless dozens of Facebook friends who have played such a pivotal part in my journey of discovery. And how about that cover art and graphics by my son, Nick! I am so proud of him! Last, but definitely not least, I could not have done this without the valuable advice and guidance from my editorial team; Jen, Andy, Jami, Lexi, and Liz.

Chapters

Acknowledgements: v

Forward ix

The Power of Sincere (Seemingly Unimportant) Conversations xi
    My Role as a Writer xx

Introduction. xxi
    Life Comes in Thirds xxii

One: Hot Ashes for Trees. 1

Two: Finally, The End of the End Times 24

Three: The Doctrine of Hell and Eternal Separation 57

Four: Re-thinking My Inherited Beliefs. 71

Five: What About Bible Inerrancy? 112

Six: Birth Canal Memories. 134

Seven: The Late Pickers 173

Eight: Field of Grasshoppers. 188

Forward

By Joshua Tongol (author of "So You Thought You Knew")

Field of Grasshoppers is not only an autobiography of Ken Dahl's theological and spiritual journey, but it's also the story of millions around the world who have grown up within institutional Christianity.

As I read through this manuscript, I couldn't help but notice the similarities of our stories. Like Ken, I grew up in fear (the scaredy-cat kind) of God for many years. I was also driven by legalism. And I had a big disconnect between what I *believed* in my head and what I really believed in my heart. That is why I appreciate this book so much. It speaks my heart. It asks the questions I would ask. And it inspires people to think for themselves.

Sure, some of Ken's ideas might make some readers feel uncomfortable—and possibly even upset. But I'm also willing to bet that it will make others—who are tired of religion—feel a sense of spiritual liberation for the very first time. One doesn't have to agree with all of Ken's conclusions to appreciate the brutal honesty he displays throughout the entire book. Like most of us, I'm sure he doesn't enjoy being wrong at times. But what I admire about him is that he is willing to admit the fact when he is. And still … he keeps moving forward.

That, my friend, is the heart of a true seeker.

Thankfully, this isn't an angry book against religion. Instead, it's a valuable, thought-provoking piece of work, which promotes love, truth and unity—the very things I see exemplified in Ken's interactions with people in real life.

So whatever questions you may have at the moment, I encourage you face them head on. There's no need to be afraid. Acknowledge your doubts. Be excited to learn. And continue to pursue the truth—no matter what the cost. And if you're willing to step out of your comfort zone as you read on, then you'll soon realize that there is a lot more truth to discover along this journey. A lot more indeed.

The Power of Sincere (Seemingly Unimportant) Conversations

This section contains a select few of the many statements of support I have received from around the world for the development of this book. I sincerely wish I could have included them all (more can be viewed at facebook.com/fieldofgrasshoppers).

About three years prior to writing this book I began simply sharing from my heart several of the aspects of my personal journey. At first I thought to myself, "There must be others out there who are able to relate to my experiences." I had no idea at the time that my short, little seemingly unimportant articles would resonate so strongly, not with a handful of people, but with thousands. What started as one man sharing his journey with a few friends on Facebook turned into a more than obvious demand for a book that could eventually be beneficial to even more people around the world who were hungry for this same message.

What we all have to say is more valuable to others than we might think. My dear, appreciated readers, you are so beautiful and so significant! You have so much to offer just by speaking your heart! No one's light is like your light. No one's expression is your expression! The rest of the world needs your thoughts, your feelings, and your stories. Your points of view that you think are silly or irrelevant could actually be extremely valuable gifts to others. Please allow what has transpired in the comments of support below – to show you that there are no *little, unimportant stories*.

Steve Olive, from Dayton, Ohio:

> The reason this book is so impressive to me is because Ken is not afraid to ask the hard questions about religion. For many, his brutal honesty is scary, but to me a breath of fresh air. For those who have been wearing the mask of religious performance this book asks all the questions that most wish they could ask but do not have the guts to pose for fear of rejection. If you desire more than religion and seek honesty with yourself and fellow man then this book is a must read.

Jim Marjoram, from Warkworth, New Zealand:

> Ken's relentless quest for spiritual integrity has challenged me to consistently ask the hard questions, not be afraid of the answers, and be willing to have my paradigms shifted.

Sharon Palmer Tucker, from Monroe, North Carolina:

> Ken Dahl has written here what I, as a pastor myself for many years, feel is a truth that is unavoidable in our generation. When you move past your fears and preconceived ideas, you understand deeply that we have to let what is unfolding within people, all over the world, shape its own form — Spirit. It will define itself. I don't know about you, but I am embracing the New Wine Skin of this day.
>
> The first few times I read Ken's work, I came like Nicodemus at night, didn't want anyone to see me. But after I began to process what was being said, I realized Ken was boldly going where no man dared go, but wanted to, answering the tough questions that I had secretly asked myself, but never voiced. Almost instantly, God became *bigger* than I had ever known, and I was *free* from *fear*. Finally, I could *exhale*; I was *free*, after decades of the narrow boundaries of religious tradition.

THE POWER OF SINCERE (SEEMINGLY UNIMPORTANT) CONVERSATIONS

Debbie Ann Ward, from Port Macquarie, New South Wales:

> Ken Dahl has always been one place I could feel safe to be me, and say the things my own heart needed to say. It has never been the things I knew that transformed me, but the things I didn't; and those things I was never taught in church but learnt through joining conversations. The mind that got me into trouble is never the same mind that gets me out. ~ 12 step slogan.

Hilda Beukes, from South Africa:

> Ken encourages people to come together with open minds, he voices what a lot of us are already thinking or feeling and provokes thoughtful conversation on subjects we should have been discussing a long time ago. I have such a great appreciation for how he inspires a world of love, compassion and gratitude.

Jen Fishburne, from Houston, Texas:

> What if we are asking the wrong questions when we read the Bible? Will we end up with the wrong answers? Has the church unnecessarily complicated the simple truths that Jesus taught? Ken Dahl opens his heart as he shares his own personal journey in *Field of Grasshoppers* in learning to ask different questions and finds some surprising answers to life on planet earth today. I did not expect to find myself in tears at the end of Ken's story. Everyone who has ever read the Bible needs to do themselves a favor and consider looking at the Bible from a slightly different angle as Ken takes us on a journey to find real life.

Peter Overduin, from Capelle aan den IJssel, Netherlands:

> On the basis of logic and nature I came by many of the same thoughts as Ken has. Because of my religious background, however, I dared not believe that what my heart had always tried to tell me was the truth. Ken's work on theological reform has helped me to overcome the fear of logical and natural principles, and trusting my own God given intuition. Not all Christian theology comes from the heart of God. Ken's work helped me understand that.

Licette Lofgren, from Sweden:

> When I came across Ken's writings I understood that I was not alone on this journey and it became easier to trust my thoughts, feelings and insights that God is so much more easy and natural than we think. I knew that there was so much more and kept on searching until I realized that it is only unconditional love that sets us free, my mind opened up and saw that a religious mindset is not the way.

Paul Townsend, from Georgia:

> In our dogmatic, 'ask no questions' religions, God is posed as a separate, somewhat emotional, human-like, spirit being that resides outside of us, a 'ghost' running the 'machine' of what we call reality. Is this dualism really Truth, or are we something else entirely? What secrets lie behind the veil? Follow along with Ken Dahl as he dares to question the unquestionable. You will not be disappointed!

Shirley Lincoln, from Gig Harbor, Washington:

> My friendship with Ken has blessed me with the pleasure and honor of witnessing and learning from his transformation. I have grown spiritually and emotionally from his freedom and honesty about his personal journey of spiritual and philosophical ascension. I have learned that it all starts with changing ourselves. I am so incredibly grateful for Ken's contribution to our world.

THE POWER OF SINCERE (SEEMINGLY UNIMPORTANT) CONVERSATIONS

Sharon Osborne, from South Africa (South Coast):

> Ken sure has encouraged me in my lonesome walk to freedom. When I discovered his voice in the wilderness I realized I was not alone, and I was not insane.

Byron Mill, from Redcliffe, Queensland, Australia:

> I have followed Ken's work for almost a year now and I have gone from a pure skeptic of his ideas to understanding and embracing what he shares along his journey of discovery. I find Ken giving voice to my inner questions, and his words are always edifying, giving me those "aha" moments. *Field of Grasshoppers* is definitely a book I will read more than once.

Margi Wilmans, from Kwambonambi, Kwazulu-Natal, South Africa:

> These were words reaching a fearful, severely brainwashed and, for lack of a better word, crusty being. At times I would switch the computer off unable to absorb any more of Ken's writings. I would always go back with a new curiosity to see what else he had written. A light was somehow beginning to shine through, immobilizing some of my darkest fears. I found myself shedding layers of religious fear and beginning to really breathe life again. Here I am a couple of years later, so grateful for people like Ken who never wavered in seeking the truth on this wonderful journey of spiritual freedom. My inherited 'hell fire,' 'submit to authority or else,' fear-driven, 'rebellion is as witchcraft,' obligation based religion is finally gone.

Frank Speer, from Ocala, Florida:

> Remember the carefree joys and freedoms of early childhood? Who says we can't go back? Ken Dahl is not afraid to grapple with life's biggest and best questions. For many, reading *Field of Grasshoppers* will be like being set free from a sort of bondage, the grey clouds will part, the shimmering sunlight will come blazing through, and you will understand how to truly relish

life. Allow Ken's personal journey and unique insights to lift you out of the mire and into the light of restoration, purpose and invigoration. -- Frank Speer, Author and Host of The Frank Show podcast, (frankshow.org).

Andre' van der Merwe, from Johannesburg, Gauteng, South Africa:

When I first stumbled upon Ken's writings, I was stunned. I had never witnessed someone think about God that far outside the 'Christian box' before. But once I got over my initial caution, Ken helped me to realize that my intellect and my heart were not my enemies. If you are someone who is not afraid of finding skeletons in the closet of your beliefs, I highly recommend *Field of Grasshoppers* -- it's the ride of a lifetime!

Alice Fiorelli Russo, from Berlin, New Jersey:

Everything worth knowing, worth believing in, comes from within. We already know the truth but we struggle to trust and believe our own inner-knowing. Thank you Ken, for being faithful to that Inner Voice above all. Thank you for not only knowing it and living it, but also for sharing it and teaching it. Thank you for your support and encouragement as I take the necessary steps to shake loose the remaining shackles of a religious mind-set. This book is a real gift. Open it and receive the confirmation you crave for the secret knowing you already hold within your own heart.

Venessa Seagreen, from White River, Mpumalanga, South Africa:

I have learned more from the contents of this book than thirty years in the church, and I am closer to God now than I have ever been – now that I am finally able to use my brain and logic. The last few years have been the most amazing life-transforming ones of my entire life. This incredible journey with Ken has changed me from a fear driven Pentecostal Christian to someone who's entire view of who God and life itself has changed for the better and created a hunger in me of who I really am. Just when you think you know it all, Ken drops the next bombshell forcing me to rethink everything that has been fed to me my whole life.

Kim Harvey, from Boston, Massachusetts:

Ken started the conversations, threw in logic, reason, whit, and humor, invoking crazed anger, paralyzing fear, a heartbeat skip, utter joy, choking laughter, and the inevitable crack in cemented religious dogma.

Doug Torkelson, from Tulsa, Oklahoma:

Ken is one of the most fearless warrior-seeker-questioners I have ever met. If reincarnation was true, and I could pick a handful of people to help me through the maze of religion/spirituality in the next life, I would definitely pick Ken to be on my team. Come to think of it, maybe I did. I love his honest, thoughtful, deep reflections and challenges. If you have doubts about some of your religious beliefs but are afraid to move forward, this book is for you. Ken has a wonderful way of asking tough, probing questions about things you probably have pondered. Many people will be able to relate to these stories and insights. This book, *Field of Grasshoppers,* is going to dramatically change Ken's life, as well as the life of many others.

Jay Redinger, from Shelly Beach, Kwazulu-Natal, South Africa:

For too long the Christian world has simply accepted the religious dogma handed down from previous generations, without ever challenging its validity. Ken's contribution, *Field of Grasshoppers,* is about to change all that. He will make you think, not necessarily what to think, but most definitely to think. His ability to appeal to your God given logic and your intuitive ability to recognize truth is astounding. Don't be surprised if some of your favorite long held beliefs start unraveling at the seams and being replaced with a freedom that comes from seeking the truth.

Dotty Pratt, from Gresham, Oregon:

> If you have always had more questions than answers about your religion and are hungry to share those questions with like-minded folks who won't judge you, then you will find Ken's book not only satisfying, but a great jumping off board to a journey you've longed for and perhaps also feared. Ken has a unique gift for putting into words so many of the things that others of us think and feel as well. I am so grateful that Ken has shared that gift. Let your Faith be bigger than your fears. It's not so hard when you find you are not alone.

Steve Elsmore, from Grand Junction, Colorado:

> "To infinity and beyond," *Field of Grasshoppers* will take you there, and the strange part is that you will understand how you got there. Ken's work has drawn me out of complacent acceptance and transported me to a place where I can rethink many of the traditional dogmatic views I held. I strongly recommend everyone read *Field of Grasshoppers* and allow yourself to actually consider the thoughts he so clearly lays out, you may find you also change and become free.

Cynthia Linox, from Dallas, Texas:

> Most of what Ken has shared on spiritual enlightenment has provoked me to question EVERYTHING I've learned in church. Not only do I question it all, I refute most of the traditional religious doctrines I've been taught. Amazing how I've been awakened to a truth that's brought much freedom to our lives. I've learned so much from Ken in such a short time, more than the twenty five years I spent in church. More than anything else, I've learned to think for myself!

THE POWER OF SINCERE (SEEMINGLY UNIMPORTANT) CONVERSATIONS

Colin Lagerwall, from Newcastle, KwaZulu-Natal:

> Dear Reader ... Our job in this generation is to try to find the answers to the posed questions of previous generations, and likewise, when we have found some answers, to rewrite the questions based on our renewed understanding. Ken has not in any way been reticent in doing his job; in fact, he has asked the unquestionable questions that many have not even dared to allow themselves to think...
>
> I have shared some of Ken's writings with my fellow 'congregants', and they have had their worlds turned right side up, so be prepared to let go of the 'old wine skin' that cannot be stretched anymore, and enjoy the time of Your life as you get to burst in wonder from the inside out at the new understandings that Ken presents, of questions answered with truths that have probably been here since time began.

Amie May, from San Antonio, Texas:

> Ken Dahl boldly asks what you were thinking, and validates what you know in your heart to be true. In the least, his message will give you things to think and talk about. At most, it will save your life.

My Role as a Writer

It is not the books being written by people like myself that are changing the world, but the conversations that they are creating. All I am doing here is starting a conversation. What the last generation avoided at all costs is having full and fearless discussions on the subjects they did not want to talk about, or even think about. This generation is different. They are saying, "Yes, we are having these conversations! And what's more, we are going to fully investigate every possible angle and viewpoint until we get to the bottom of it all!"

The book you are about to read was not written by a seasoned Bible scholar with a doctorate degree in Christian theology, but just a regular guy sitting across the table from you at your local coffee shop. The following is a true story of a journey that is currently being taken by millions of people just like me. I have merely given them all a voice…

Introduction

"All of man's trouble stems from his inability to sit quietly in a room alone." —Blaise Pascal

This is so true. I have always relished my time alone out in nature. It is indeed where most of life's questions can be answered. And yet, if I am to be honest, I have not always wanted all of my questions answered.

There is something natural about life, about the seasons of life, and even about God. As a child, my intuition told me that life's most significant mysteries can be solved without libraries full of books on theology. At a very young age, there was an obvious simplicity, an almost knowing, that all the hidden answers were going to somehow roll out in front of me like a soft, summer picnic blanket as I grew older. I don't know why or how I knew this: I just did.

Then came the teachers, preachers, politicians, business mentors, and all the combined ego-based messages from society, not just to tell me that nature doesn't hold the answers, but that it is actually the enemy. Little by little, my real world of enchantment and simplicity was replaced with a long list of largely dysfunctional human illnesses. In no time at all, my self-worth and self-actualization were based upon competition, obligation, inferiority, exclusionism, guilt, shame, fear, self-doubt, self-righteousness, self-abasement, religious arrogance, philosophical and education-based pride, financial security, occupation and status, materialism and acquisition. The list is endless of what mankind offers us in exchange for our souls. One of my most treasured mentors, Marianne Williamson, puts it this way: "It's as though, as soon as we got here, we were given a sleeping pill. The thinking of the world, which is not based on love, began pounding in our ears the moment we hit shore."

Life Comes in Thirds

During our younger years, we are incessantly questioning everything the establishment throws our way. Then there are the middle years, when we have pretty much settled into most of it, even as odd as some of it seems. School, occupation, recreation, and our social life takes up our time and energy, leaving us with very little reason or desire to even question what we have long since accepted as truth. When we get older, we return to our childlike state, once again asking a never-ending list of questions. However, the difference then is that we are no longer asking how things are, but whether or not what we've been taught is correct or not. At this point, we have had the time to think about all the ideologies, philosophies, and doctrines, and see how they compare to the real world we've been living in. Some of it fits, some of it sort of fits, but we begin to realize that a bunch of it doesn't fit at all. Such was the case for me.

I'm returning to innocence. Don't try to stop me.

ONE

HOT ASHES FOR TREES

"You must be changed back into little children…" (Matthew 18:3, paraphrased) —Jesus

The field of freshly cut hay partly shadowed by puffy September clouds spread out majestically in front of the six-year-old boy like a blanket called God. With adventure in his eyes, he slipped through the wire-tied cattle gate and ran toward the beckoning trees at the end of the small lake behind the barn. The forest, as usual, had been impatiently waiting all morning for his presence. The chatter of flying grasshoppers rose in front of him like the fanfare of faithful subjects at the sound of his royal, approaching feet. At the forest's edge, he stopped and spun around for a glance back at the farmhouse. With his arms outstretched, he looked straight up at a small flock of circling swallows, closed his eyes, and inhaled the late morning fragrances of autumn. Life would never get any better than this, he thought to himself. And he was right; and he was wrong.

That is how it all started out: simple, innocent, and free. I learned that the stove was hot, thin ice is dangerous; I needed to keep my distance from the bee's nest, and never attempt to pet a porcupine. Don't play with matches, look both ways before crossing the road, and always have an exit strategy when the family bull squared off with me for using his field as a shortcut to the lake. That just about covers my survival training as a boy growing up on a farm.

That's Just the Way It Is

Parents know that harder life lessons are on their way so they do the best they can, with the knowledge their generation has provided, to prepare us for those challenges. Somewhere, around age eight, I had become accustomed to having most of my questions met with convincing answers from my parents. Most of those questions were two-word sentences: "But why?" I began to notice that my parents were also relying on outside sources for many of their life answers. And so, at a very young age, I surmised that since I can safely believe what my loving parents said, then I could also rely on what their outside sources were saying. Consequently, most of what I ended up formulating as truth was not learned through self-discovery, but inherited from the people I trusted. I think that is true for most people.

During this time, my parents' outside source was a small Pentecostal church on the edge of town. They believed in the operation of the gifts of the Spirit, one of those gifts being that speaking in tongues was the evidence of being filled with God's Spirit. We were told that being filled with the Holy Ghost would give us the power to live a more victorious life. It was also supposedly evidence that we were living in the last days, all based on the Bible of course. Like many other Christian organizations, our denomination tried their absolute best to interpret the Bible as accurately as they could, drawing upon many well-renowned theologians with the highest reputation of biblical integrity possible. Like every other church in town, we thought we had the purest interpretation of the scriptures.

Although my theological beliefs now greatly differ from the church doctrines I grew up learning, I remain extremely grateful for the life sustaining Christian principles my parents taught me. Truth be known, my mom was the best 'pastor' I have ever known. If there were a way of knowing the extent of the generational impact her work as a Sunday school teacher has had over the years, the number of people would probably fill an arena.

Confessions of a Former Pentecostal Christian

The following few pages are about my personal experience and evolving theological perspective growing up with a Pentecostal background. It is important for me to stress that I am grateful for all the mentors in my life: from my parents, to my pastors, to Bible college professors, all of which were an enormous influence in my life. Some of my story is about asking very tough questions, and coming to some quite shocking conclusions for myself. I want to assure the reader that my theological journey of discovery is not about a man who was socially wounded by uncaring clergy or church members. Most pastors and parishioners I have known throughout my life have been some of the most caring, loving, selfless people I have ever met. I have several close family members who are currently involved in very meaningful church ministries. Their contributions and commitments of helping others are significant, and I sincerely applaud them for that. I do not have to agree with their theology in order to commend them for being passionate about making a difference in the world.

You'll Never Fall in Love, Young Man

It was 1969 in Hibbing, Minnesota, and an uncomfortably humid summer night in the house of God. The thick air was broken by the soft sound of crinkling paper as the older women fanned their faces with the evangelist's fliers. With his Bible held high above his head, he paced theatrically back and forth across our church's modest little stage. I remember watching with focused intensity as the ceiling fan gently flipped through the thin pages. The out of breath, traveling preacher screamed out, "Jesus is coming sooonnnn*ah*! And we winnnn*ah*! I rrread the last chapterrr*ah*!!! Glory to God *ah*!" His body twisted in perfect timing with his accentuated "*ah*" exclamation points. The congregation of the faithful was responding with an almost visual wave of romantic tears and raised hands unto the Lord. "Thank you, Jesus! Thank you, Jesus!" an elderly lady cried out with the most unforgettable look of sweet relief that she very soon would be seeing the King of Kings, face-to-face, as the skies above our little town would roll back and the last trumpet would sound. The impassioned orator in the sweat-soaked shirt became emotional as he purposely fell to one knee. He stared directly at me, wiping his face with a towel, assuring the congregation that the coming of the Lord was only five to ten years away, and most definitely not twenty.

I was thirteen years old, and I suddenly knew that I would never fall in love. The only thing that really mattered now was saving the lost from an eternal, burning lake of fire. I couldn't let that happen to my friends. I knew right then what I had to do, and that was to invite them to these special meetings before the evangelist left town. If I neglected to do my part, they might be lost forever. I had also stopped applying myself in school. My rationale was, "What difference is it going to make in heaven if I can add and subtract fractions?" My situation was not unique, for these same sermons were being authoritatively proclaimed with the same 'Holy Ghost anointed' vigor in churches all across our fruited plains. Most of the Sunday morning sermons were actually full of life changing principles, which somehow validated the significantly flawed, sensational stuff. The pastor and his wife were such wonderful people who loved and cared about their congregation. We adored and trusted their leadership in the same way a child trusts his loving parents. If the end times preaching were simply a passing sensational craze, it wouldn't have mattered much. As church history would soon sadly prove, this "end of the world is near" message would become even more popular as the years rolled on. As current news events were weaved into the preaching, they added yet another level of fear and unrest to the mix, and our interest level only intensified.

You'll Never Have Children of Your Own

At age fifteen, I knew that I would never get married or experience the joys of fatherhood, but I had come to the understanding that we Christians were like some exclusive race of humans who may be sucked up into the sky at any time without warning. We were all led to believe that this doctrine was based on ancient Bible text. No one in the church, in 1970, knew that the doctrine of pre-tribulation rapture had never been found in history before 1830, or that it was first promoted by an Irish minister named John Nelson Darby. It went from there to Cyrus I. Scofield (Scofield Reference Bible) to the Moody Bible Institute, and then Hal Lindsey's book became the greatest evangelical tool in church history promoting the futurist eschatology that most evangelical churches now teach as biblical fact. We know that now, but we didn't know it then.

When I was sixteen, in 1972, the fear-designed church movie called *A Thief in the Night* was being played night after night in churches all across America in the hopes of scaring people into the kingdom. That film was followed by three sequels and a novel, laying the marketing foundation for the end times film and book industry, which fizzled out in the late 70s only to resurface again (ironically) twenty years later in the 1990s with movies like *Apocalypse*, *The Rapture*, *Left Behind*, and several others, all warning of the imminent return of Jesus, which was continually being proven wrong decade after decade after decade.

Pounding the Point Over

Like any eighteen-year-old, I wanted my freedom, and being free from having to go to church three times a week was a big part of that. So I joined the army in the hopes of getting away and seeing the world. I ended up in Germany as a combat engineer by day and a drug dealer by night. After six years of living in a drug-induced dream, there wasn't much left of the innocent boy who was once inviting his friends to come see the scary evangelist with the fresh, new insights on the book of Revelation.

My long road to full recovery placed me back at that little church on the edge of town, and before long, I was right back where I thought I belonged. Deep inside I always believed I was meant for something great, like being a part of a revolution that was going to change the world. So, my wife and I, and our two little boys, pulled up in front of North Central Bible College in downtown

Minneapolis. I stood there on the sidewalk in reverential, but idealistic, awe as I gazed upwards at those aged, vine-covered brick buildings, thinking to myself, "How many great and noble men of God has this gospel factory produced? This is the place where my life's meaning and purpose is all going to come together!" But I was wrong.

To me, Bible College didn't seem like a place where young people go to learn how to be more open-minded and question all things, but rather a place to establish a highly romanticized version of what our denomination had already taught us. One's religious upbringing could be compared to hammering a nail through a wall and Bible College represented going around and pounding the exposed point over. It is a place where you learn not to question what your home pastor taught, and that out of all the denominations in the world, this one is unquestionably the most biblically accurate. However, as the semesters rolled by, my heart began to fight with my head, not only with certain doctrines but also with the whole 'us vs. them' mentality of modern Christianity. No matter how spiritually romantic it was worded, it always felt like, "We who have the love must go out and minister to those who don't have the love." And although it made sense to my doctrine-formatted head, it all seemed strangely odd to my heart. I remember being sent out from an evangelism class in what they called a 'street ministry,' armed with key questions and verses in hopes of collecting as many sinners' prayers from homeless people as we could. The following day, students would stand up in class and share testimonies of their evangelism 'successes.' This grieved my heart deeply because I knew that by simply using homeless people to sharpen our evangelism skills, we were hurting more people than we were helping, not to mention cementing in some of their minds that this version of Christianity lacks the real heart of the 'Jesus' we were supposedly following, and representing.

God Never Changes, But Yes, We Do

Our generation is a very small slice of time compared to the entire history of the Christian church. We all tend to view our particular place in history as the 'finally enlightened ones.' Yet if we were honest enough to showcase even the last half-century of our church's changes, a book would be produced of which we would not want anyone else to read. While exploring what the next fifty years may have in store, let us take a trip down memory lane of the last fifty years in America's Pentecostal churches.

1960s

If a Sunday school teacher was spotted standing in line at the movie theater, she would be getting a visit from the elders of the church informing her that she could no longer teach children about Jesus. What movie in 1960 could have possibly warranted that punishment? The same would have happened to the woman who dared to attend church wearing a dress that revealed her knees. When I was eight years old I got my backside tanned by the pastor's wife because I twisted my feet on a newspaper to rip it. She thought I was doing the twist. I distinctly remember church members looking down their noses at a divorced woman with two kids who showed up in church with her new boyfriend. Most churches did not accept interracial marriage. Two adult women holding hands would have been physically escorted out of the building.

1970s

Jesus didn't return before 1970 like we all believed He would. I remember how even the charismatic churches were very leery of adding a drum set or electric guitar to the song service. They were saying rock music had that evil jungle beat that mesmerizes the youth. Jesus didn't return in 1975 as Jack Van Impe had projected. Also, am I the only one who remembers hearing about the demon of alcohol or the demon of lust? And what about the Shekinah Glory, which was romanced as some sort of Holy Ghost wind that would supposedly blow in through the church windows and doors when corporate worship reached a certain spiritual crescendo? I distinctly remember one particular time, comically looking back, that the church furnace kicking on was momentarily mistaken for something else. I think the 70's could quite fittingly be called the 'signs and wonders years.'

When the Student Is Not Ready

> "It's out there somewhere, way past the sunset line. Way out on the open road." – Chris Rea

At age thirty, I returned to my childhood homestead, realizing that the world, which had evolved around me, didn't even come close to the fearless adventurism or the inquisitive, childlike freedom I had remembered experiencing on that farm. Actually, it all seemed to be going unnaturally in just the opposite direction, into a twisted and regimentally defined, man-made world of barriers, filters, and regulators of reality. Life had somewhere along the line become full of rules and guidelines all mixed together with the intimidation of allowing others to define who and what I am. This was anything but beautiful and innocent. My adult life could more accurately be described as awkward, constrictive, and unnatural. My beauty had been painted with fear, my innocence with guilt, and my freedom with religion-based indebtedness. What made Christianity so confusing to me was that the church's theology was a mixture of the true and beautiful, with the crazy and ugly. Some of the teachings were obviously correct, and even life changing, but my heart somehow always knew that some of it couldn't possibly be true.

I trudged through the tall grass and small forest that used to be our front yard. "This used to be my playground," I said to myself. Now it was but a faint memory of a childlike confidence I had long since been convinced to no longer trust. I stumbled clumsily across the uneven, brush-infested ground, making my way to a much-needed view of the lake, but the lake was gone. It looked more like a small, dried-up swamp. "How is that possible?" I thought. The once-beckoning forest seemed to say, nothing. I thought to myself, if those towering pines could talk, they would probably say, "We don't recognize who you are anymore."

I found no clues or inspiration standing there on that narrow gravel road. I carelessly concluded that following my heart out to that old, abandoned property was a waste of time. As I opened my car door for the long drive home, I said to myself, "Well, that's life." But is it really? Another twenty years would pass, before I was even able to seriously question whether or not the magical land of my childhood was an actual picture of how we were intended to live our entire lives all along.

1980s

Parishioners were strongly discouraged from seeking secular professional counseling, church leadership exhorting us rather to seek divine healing in front of the church podium. Oh, and Jesus didn't return before 1982 as Hal Lindsey told us he would. The book entitled *88 Reasons The Rapture Will be in 1988* by Edgar C. Wisenant also slipped conveniently into the sea of Christian forgetfulness. Since Hal's 1982 prediction failed, he publicly signed onto Whisenant's new date, based upon Israel becoming a State in 1948, which was interpreted as the blossoming of the fig tree; therefore the generation that sees that 1948 event would be the generation that would not pass away until Jesus returns. Hence, a generation, being 40 years, places the rapture somewhere around 1988. After the passing of the deadline in 88 Reason's, Mr. Whisenant came out with a new book called *89 Reasons why the Rapture is in 1989*. This book sold only a fraction of his prior release. This was followed by a book called *When Your Money Fails* by Colin Deal, which promised to "prove beyond a shadow of a doubt" that we were indeed living in the last moments of time on earth in 1988. Oops.

By the late 1980s, this subject moved from Sunday morning to Sunday night. By the 1990s, it moved from Sunday night to Wednesday night. In the early 2000s, it moved from Wednesday night out into thin air, where it all but disappeared from most church bulletins. Some in church leadership felt that since the Book of Revelation is so difficult to decipher and can only lead to dissension among the saints, it should be something that is only discussed in some obscure, small-group Bible study. The mindset of church leadership was, "If we don't shelve it as an 'it doesn't matter as long as we're ready' issue, we could lose members over it."

By this time, the loud and boisterous claims of the '70s and '80s about the imminent return of Jesus, obviously proving not to be imminent, became somewhat of an unspoken embarrassment. Did someone step up boldly to a microphone and report their realization of being wrong? No. They simply changed the subject from "Jesus is coming soon" to "We need to be ready even if He doesn't come soon," and many pastors stopped preaching on the subject altogether. I can't say that I blame them.

The Gift of Knowledge

Although there had been obscure traveling evangelists, a few of which obviously had some sort of God-given clairvoyant gift of knowledge, it was Pat Robertson who really made this practice popular by boldly showcasing it on every episode of the 700 Club. Mr. Robertson, with tightly closed eyes, saying things like, "I see a family somewhere in Michigan," over the next twenty years turned into many televangelists saying the same things, and especially when trading miracles for money to support their ministries. What disturbed me more than that was the fact that both pastors and parishioners kept timidly silent about such embarrassing, and obviously wrong behavior. Televangelists were like the bad child that the family just didn't talk about. But by not talking about it, the world outside the church translated the silence as endorsement.

1990s

I remember being sternly warned by people in the church that I should be very careful of saying anything negative about televangelists, because I might unknowingly be slandering one of God's anointed. The warning alluded that I could actually be in physical harm for doing so. Taking communion with the wrong attitude was also thought to be a thing of possible danger. Oh, and Jesus didn't return before 1992 as Jack Van Impe's newest prediction had reported. The late '90s can also be justifiably marked as the decade where so many of us found ourselves hinging a great deal of our self-esteem on having a daily impressive testimony of how God either talked to us or used us in a spiritual ministry of some capacity. Everyone had a ministry, you know, like the apostle Paul. It defined us as useful and significant to both our peers and ourselves. We do not like to admit this quirky, psychologically unbalanced stuff, but it was indeed a part of our church history.

The Sign Holders

From the days of D. L. Moody all the way up through last Wednesday on the corner of 348th and Pacific Highway in Federal Way, Washington, evangelical Christians have been holding warning signs at busy intersections. The most popular ones are "Turn or Burn," and "Repent and Be Saved," and "Jesus is coming soon/Are you ready?" and "Heaven or Hell, Your Choice." Most evangelicals of today view this foolish, minority mode of evangelical communication as a lack of good judgment, or an unfortunate embarrassment for the church, or even as activity that hurts the cause of Christ more than it helps. However, what they fail to do is connect the dots of the incorrect doctrines that made such "us vs. them" zealotry so easy to have happened. The theology seldom gets blamed, mainly because most evangelicals actually agree with the words on most of those signs, you know, the same signs that they are embarrassed about.

Look Around, Choose Your Own Ground

Over time we all observe what is going on around us. We all notice the cultural and social changes, but we don't always grasp the hows and whys of those changes. Although the church did have a benevolent heart toward the downtrodden, their main mission seemed to be offering eternal life insurance policies to escape God's soon coming judgment on this sinking ship called Earth. No one ever stopped to think thoughts like, "Okay, so, one of the main reasons we are here is to get safely to somewhere else? Huh?"

By this time in American history, evangelical Christianity had all but removed their influence from such culture forming institutions like state colleges, politics, and even local community organizations. The driving (subconscious) rationale was that there simply wasn't enough time left to change the world. "We are not of this world" was the proverbial mantra, as we zealously readied the life rafts for the 'soon coming' prophetic storm. Twenty years later, the church stood surprised that non-churchgoing folks had taken the helm of our country's culture building institutions. We abandoned our role as the salt of the earth and the light of the world for the foolishness of going into the lifeboat (rapture) business. The results are obvious. Who does the church blame? Hollywood, the devil, and in some evangelical circles, even the democrats.

"Ken, Don't You Miss the Unction?"

Recently I was asked how I now process my experience in the Pentecostal culture. The person asking wanted to know how I can now just "discard that Pentecostal infilling experience," and the "thunderous moves of the Spirit in those services," and the "unction you feel that simply cannot be explained away." These are all very sincere questions. I was raised in the Assemblies of God denomination, and yes, I have experienced many of the highly emotional and unexplainable things they practice, including speaking or praying in tongues.

I come from a culture of people who were nurtured from an early age to not only want, but to need, the miraculous on an almost daily basis. In my honest opinion, this actually happens, or appears to happen, mostly because they themselves are manufacturing and manifesting such a lifestyle via the Law of Attraction. It evolves quickly from "I think I am hearing from God," to "God spoke to me and said," or "I had a dream last night," or "I had a vision, and God showed me," or "As Cheryl was talking to me, I saw in the spirit that she was depressed," or "On my way to the store the Lord placed you on my heart." So, even basic human intuition was often translated as, "God showed me something." After all, if God can have a conversation with Moses, Noah, and Abraham, then He can talk to us on a regular basis too. Interestingly, if you want to hear from people who have conversations with God on a daily basis, the place to go is not the New Testament church record, but any local Pentecostal church in town.

The wonderful people in that culture indeed have a deeply romantic religion, and their rituals and practices are very personal and real to them. It was understood that if we corporately worshiped God sincerely enough, and sang enough songs in the right heartfelt, earnest fashion, He just may come down and visit our building today, and then the pastor can say, "Without a doubt, the Spirit of the Lord is surely in this place this morning!" I have no argument with whether individuals and groups of people can have spiritual experiences, but I am now convinced that God is no more in this place than He is at the Dairy Queen or on the surface of the moon. "God" indeed is in all three places equally. I believe that devotional, gratitude filled worship is not for God, but for us. I do not believe it moves God, I believe it moves us. The power of positive thoughts and prayers is something I believe mankind is just now beginning to understand.

Baptized in the Holy Spirit

This was that additional power the church claimed I needed to receive for a more victorious Christian life. I remember asking myself, "So are they saying that being born again isn't quite enough to keep me away from that old cocaine habit, or falling into gossip, or stop me from noticing that younger, curvaceous gal at the shopping mall?" Looking back, it is now clear to me that one could compare the general personal growth in character of many people who were said to have been baptized in the Holy Spirit with those who were not and notice very little difference. I have often asked myself, "If speaking in tongues endow a person with the power to live a more victorious life, then why wouldn't it also result in one's social maturity?" I do not say this to make fun of Pentecostals, but simply to make an intellectually honest observation that anyone can confirm. I would even go so far as to say that one's social, philosophical, mental, emotional, cultural, and even spiritual maturity is not affected significantly by praying in tongues. In my honest opinion, it is more about a romantic, emotion-based desire for experiencing the mystical and miraculous, all based on the teaching that this practice ushers you into a deeper, spiritually sacred realm. And it probably does.

In Bible College, the mandatory study of a California coast event from 1906 to approximately 1915, called the Azusa Street Revival was romanced almost to the same level as the Second Coming itself. This part of Pentecostal church history is what really kicked off the popularized big circus-sized 'revival tent meetings' of the early 1900's, which were very poplar especially in the southern states, all the way up until the early 1970's. American Indians in the southwest who practice deeper spirituality through the ancient religious practice of smoking peyote are not far from this same, transcendental dynamic. Another quite unconventional occurrence in Pentecostal circles was people falling over into an almost unconscious state (slain in the spirit) after being touched by the preacher. Although this was unlike any New Testament record of reoccurring Christian activity, it did have quite vivid, paralleling similarities with the religious practice of smoking peyote. Similar occurrences have also been seen in Hindu prayer meetings. I am now convinced it is a human phenomenon, which does not diminish the reality or the value of it. Retreating to a deeper spiritual plane because of an intense desire for the mystical and spiritual certainly has its value.

"Tongues": #1. It is real. #2. People do not realize their own possibilities when they willingly and desirously have a longing for the miraculous, mystical, spiritual, and metaphysical, with hunger, desire, need, emotion, expectation, and faith.

I believe "tongues" are... well, a human thing, which doesn't mean they are not a valuable practice or experience. It is something manifested and developed by humans, via their desire and hunger for a deeper experience, which translates into the reality of a transcendental-like retreat (much like the deeper meditation some in the East experience). Is it powerful? Absolutely, and the reason it can get very silly and show signs of humanity is because it *is* a human thing. Does the Creator of the universe "fill" people with His Spirit, which results in them spontaneously speaking in an angelic language?

Interpretation of Tongues

I have attended a lifetime of church services where I witnessed something called "interpretations of tongues." If you are not familiar with this, right in the middle of the song service or preaching, someone in the congregation bursts out speaking in an unknown language, loudly orating in an authoritative tone. Everyone in the congregation becomes very quiet, and in reverential awe, waits for the Creator of the universe to speak (in English) the interpretation of that outburst through a member of the congregation.

After forty-plus years of experiencing Pentecostal services, I have never heard an interpretation of tongues that was any more profound in substance than the message in a fortune cookie. This fact always seemed odd to me. If one were to actually record an entire year of these events they would learn that God wants to be worshiped, He savors our praises like sweet smelling incense, we are to love one another, we should reach out to the downtrodden, we should stop sinning if we want our prayers answered, God wants to use us in ministry but can't unless our hearts are right with Him, and the list goes on and on of things like this that every Christian already knows. And many times it was the same exact message the preacher was already preaching before he was so sharply interrupted (supposedly by God Himself). Consequently, the interpretation never disagreed with any of the doctrines the pastor was teaching their flock. I often asked myself, "If the preacher was teaching God's people incorrectly, wouldn't an interpretation of tongues be a reasonable way for God to address such a thing? Or does God perhaps not care if He or scripture is being misrepresented by a preacher?" Interestingly, I also remember many interpretations (of God supposedly telling His people) about the importance of being ready and prepared (like the five wise virgins in Matthew 25:2), "for the coming of the Lord is near", and "ye know not the hour or the day". Unfortunately, those messages 'from God' to that 1974 congregation did not include the people 60 and older, because they are now either 99 years old, or gone.

I have a trusted friend who is also a pastor, who shared a story about one of his colleagues who is fluent in Greek. For the purpose of his own study, he went into a Pentecostal church known for such activities, loudly, and emotionally interrupted the service by quoting John 3:16 in Greek, to which a completely off-base 'interpretation' was given by another member of the congregation. There is nothing surprising about this to those from my background. Over time it was becoming increasingly disturbing to me how most Pentecostals were unwilling to be honest about these more than obvious, hindsight observations. The solution; don't think about them, and don't talk about them.

Again, I am very grateful for my upbringing in that culture, but my gratefulness is not a contract that ensures my loyalty to doctrines and practices I have long since moved away from.

2000s

Jesus didn't return before 2000 (Y2K), like so many were making sure they were ready for, which included stocking dry goods in the basement as a sort of, you know, 'extra oil for our lamps'. Nor did Y2K trigger a computer crash induced, financial meltdown that led to bar codes being tattooed to our hands and foreheads. Jesus did not return in 2007 as Hal Lindsey's newest calculation suggested, but Hal has alternative dates going all the way up to 2048. How convenient for future book sales to his faithful followers.

In 2011, while flipping through TV channels, I landed on the elderly TV preacher John Hagee, boldly shouting how he has no doubt that "within his lifetime" the sky will open up and Jesus will come down to earth, and "Oh, what a glorious day that will be!" He also added, "And I'm no spring chicken!" The faithful stood to their feet in rapturous applauding agreement. I thought to myself, "Where have I seen this before?" What will that congregation believe when Mr. Hagee dies of old age? Well, from the history we have reviewed so far, they will probably continue believing exactly what they were told to believe.

The number of preachers who set dates over the last fifty years is too numerous to list, but here are just a few of the more popular ones:

Jack Van Impe - 1975, 1988, 1992, 2001, 2008, "soon"…

Hal Lindsey - 1982, 1988, 2007, 2048

Pat Robertson - 1982

Lester Sumrall - 1985, 1986, 2000

Benny Hinn - 1993

Kenneth Hagin - 1997 to 2000

Jerry Falwell - 2010

John Hinkle - 1994

Louis Farrakhan – 1991

Harold Camping – 1994, 2011

Shelby Corbett – 2007

Marilyn J. Agee – 2007

Michael Drosnin (author of *The Bible Code*) - 2012

The Jehovah's Witnesses (too many dates to list)

Ellen G. White, founder of the Seventh Day Adventist church (too many to list)

Most evangelical Christians don't really keep track of things like this. Have you ever wondered why? Even after all these repeated failed predictions, Christians continue to buy their latest (revised) books. Somehow the church manages to continue the last days' urgency of an imminent event that will always be 'just around the corner,' and could happen 'any day now.'

Is it a coincidence that over the last fifty years they have all been wrong? I began wondering if it wasn't merely the date or season they had wrong, but the entire story. And yet, somehow we just kept listening to them? I thought to myself, "Forty years from now (2054), when Jesus still hasn't broken through the afternoon clouds, will we finally be ready to rethink how we've interpreted the Bible on these matters?" It is encouraging to see a trend of an increasing number of clergy willing to acknowledge that the wisdom, revelation, and even the original language and intent of the scriptures is unfolding with time. So many things in the church have changed just in the last few decades, and not just within culture but within doctrines as well.

Great Scott, I Think We Have Actually Done It!

With noble motives, people have searched the scriptures trying to figure out God, and all of the spiritual dynamics of living here on this planet. That's a good thing. Part of where I believe we may have gotten a little unbalanced is when mankind woke up one morning and said, "Great Scott, I think we have actually done it!" Not only did man's arrogant need for literary and interpretive control discolor God into a corner, but also established in the minds of the flock the elite exegetical authority of church leadership. Yet in truth, as I've already stated, this is a continually evolving process that has been unfolding for centuries. Incidentally, "what the Bible says" very often means what we think the Bible says (as church history itself has so vividly shown us all by now).

Interpretations are Interpretations

In the church culture I grew up in, when someone presented theology that differed from ours, we immediately assumed they were disagreeing with the Bible itself. Any information that differed from our long-held interpretations actually seemed crazy to us. The rationale was, "What could those people on the outside of our spiritually enlightened camp possibly see that we don't?" Recently a devout Christian lady told me the reason she knows her church's doctrines are correct is because when she reads her Bible, she asks the Holy Spirit to show her the truth in everything she studies. I simply replied, "That is a good policy, but have you ever wondered, over the last twenty years, why the Holy Spirit has never once disagreed with the doctrines of your church or your pastor? With a pastor like that, who needs the Holy Spirit?"

At one point in my life, I arrived at a place where I was finally willing to start questioning the things I had been taught. I was finally ready for the truth to differ from my truth, or for that matter, the pastor's truth. We are human beings, and we can be wrong. And yes, our pastor can be wrong, and the bible college can be wrong. And what we thought was the Holy Spirit internally confirming our church's doctrines can simply be the well-indoctrinated thoughts in our own heads, looking only for truths that agree with what we think we already know.

Moving to Seattle

Moving from deep within America's Bible belt to Seattle was quite a culture shock. One could safely say that Seattle is rich in religious culture, and that culture is a lot more tolerant of Buddhism, Taoism, metaphysical folks, and old hippies, than they are of evangelical Christians.

I took a job as a picture framer. The art industry is an occupation made up of ninety-nine percent liberal minded individuals, and the one percent, um, me, of course. This eclectic field of artisans was full of vividly expressive people, all of which I immediately stood in silent judgment of. I mentally grouped together the Buddhists and all New Age folks as spiritually lost, the liberals as thoughtless idiots, and the tattooed pot smokers with piercings as losers. I guess that was my way of, you know, 'being like Jesus'? That may have been right around the same time period when I was (strangely) convinced that if Jesus were here, he would probably be a politically-conservative Republican.

Within ten years, most of my friends were not churchgoing folks, but they were the most fun and inspiring people I had ever met. I listened to their philosophies with great interest, but always guarded myself (as trained) from adopting any of it. Again, they couldn't possibly possess anything that I needed. That's what I kept telling myself anyway. You know, the sheep and the goats: them of course being the goats. I knew that inviting them to church wasn't going to change much for them. Actually, I had the sense that it may drive an uncomfortable wedge in our relationship. And the whole idea that they needed to be like me just didn't seem natural anymore.

There was just something about all these beautiful people in my life that told me there are really big pieces missing in the whole exclusive, separatist, 'get clean and I'll be your best friend' culture of Christianity. Like many others from my church background, after a couple of decades in the real world secular work force, the culture outside the church clearly revealed itself to not be the dark, depressing, lifeless realm of the dead that preachers had painted it out to be. Why were all these worldly people just as compassionate, giving, loving, and happy as most Christians I knew? Actually, many of them clearly had a healthier self-confidence than most of my churchgoing peers. The thing that really puzzled me was that most of them were in a continual state of genuine, celebratory freedom that I only seemed to be trying to convince myself of possessing. I thought to myself, "Are we looking at the teachings of Jesus from a completely segregated point of view? Could we be gazing directly at the New Wine and actually not see it at all? Is that even possible? Was my happiness and peace of mind not to be of this world, but reserved for the afterlife?"

To Get Back Homeward

> "Once there was a way to get back homeward. Once there was a way to get back home…"
> —The Beatles

Even in my state of theological conflict, I continued attending church regularly. I began to share my frustrations with other Christians about what seemed to be a largely contradictive culture, thinking that they would certainly be able to relate. What I got back wasn't the empathy I had hoped for, but rather, they saw my questions as irreverent and my pursuit of the truth as being in danger of getting off the path. My goal wasn't about starting a new, personal religion. My fervent quest was simply about finding my way back to the little farm on that old dirt road, to regain what I had somehow lost along the way. Freedom and innocence was my hopeful destination. I can't tell you how I knew it, but I knew, in my heart of hearts, that it was out there and that I could, and would, get it back.

Sneaky Doctrine Shifters

As the years go by, theologians revisit old passages, and in recognizing their errors, reshape their flawed doctrines into more biblically accurate ones. Again, this is a very good thing. Some doctrines are completely overhauled, while others are simply readjusted. Most of us never really stop to think about it, because the changes are so slow and subtle that we don't even notice it happening. Over time, the church had changed a few doctrines without even telling us. This lack of transparency, whether intentional or not, was becoming very troubling to me.

The Doctrine of Tithing (An Indicator of Fallibility)

The once taught requirement of paying God with tithing (the Old Testament legislated amount of ten percent of one's income) has taken on new language over the last twenty years, such as the principle of tithing, or systematic giving, or covenant giving, or law of prosperity, or good stewardship, or the practice of tithing, or putting God first in your finances, and believe it or not, cheerful tithing, just to list a few. Again, no one walked up to a podium and said, "We were wrong, and we now know that God no longer requires 'faithful tithers,' but desires only 'cheerful givers.' Now, that old covenant paying has been completely replaced by new covenant giving" (2 Corinthians 9:6-14 amply replacing Malachi 3:10-11). Or do we actually need double coverage?

    The reason so many of today's churches have waxed romantic on 'tithing as a principle' is because they know that Matthew 23:23 was not even about tithing, but simply about Jesus using the Scribes and Pharisees' finest, selfish little measurements, to make a moral point about their hearts. It should also be noted that 'the others' included all the laws of Moses that they should still have been observing, as they were still (very much) under all the others. In Hebrews 7:8, Paul is addressing some Jewish Christians (in danger of returning to the Law of Moses), about the supremacy of Christ, the New High Priest, and the similarity of Christ and Melchizedek. The subject in this passage isn't just not about tithing, but Paul is clearly describing the first-century Levitical priesthood (not the Church).

    By the way, the Old Testament tithe was not something you gave, it was something you paid. We don't give our rent or mortgage payment. But again, the point here is that the church changed a long-held doctrine from authoritatively preaching it as a requirement, to then preaching it as a principle without being socially transparent enough to tell us when and why this was done. In truth, it is not a principle; it is gone, completely gone, and completely replaced (please refer to Acts 2:41-45, 4:32-35, Gal. 3:29, 2 Cor. 8:3-4, 2 Cor. 9:6-14 as billboard sized examples of what replaced it).

I thought to myself, "If they have this doctrine wrong, which they were once 'Oh, so sure' about, what else could they be wrong about? And is it acceptable for pastors to teach a certain number of blatantly false doctrines just as long as they maintain a good balance of correct doctrines?" Are these not reasonable questions? If tithing is now (all of a sudden) a principle that should be devotionally observed, then so is keeping the Sabbath holy and a long list of other observances such as feasts, special days of the year, and even the wave offering. But wait. None of those things have anything to do with financial support of the church. The fact that many churches today are still unwilling to be honest about this has greatly affected my respect for their leadership. I think that is reasonable.

Two Greatest Threats of the Church

The first thing that comes to mind for many Christians when they hear this is perhaps something atheistic in nature. Some believers' minds go directly to the moral decline of our nation as a result of movies and music that promote promiscuity and rebellion among the youth. Others, of course, will point to the political left, claiming that there is an attack on anything Christian right now in our country. And then, there are those in church leadership, who are continually warning their parishioners about the deceptive dangers of the New Age movement and those evil Eastern religions. Yet none of these are the greatest threats to the church.

The greatest threat to the church right now is actually devout, Jesus loving Christians, many of whom are seasoned Bible scholars with doctorate degrees in theology. Up until recently we have appreciated and applauded all these scholars for their service, but now they are uncovering what we never dreamed they would — that their predecessors were wrong about two very important, game-changing doctrines:

1. The Bible's version of the 'coming of the Son of Man' and the 'end of the age' (which is a completely different version than what the church has been teaching for the last 150 years).

2. The psychologically abusive doctrine of hell and eternal separation from God.

The freedom my wife and I have experienced by finally getting to the bottom of these two doctrines has proven to be the beginning of all the other ideology-based chains that have been dropping off our lives ever since.

Two

FINALLY, THE END OF THE END TIMES

I had no idea growing up in the church that there even was another widely held view of the book of Revelation among world-renowned theologians, known as the 'Preterist' view. The preterist view, which was the main, majority belief of the church for over a thousand years, placed the entire book of Revelation, and the teachings of Jesus about a judgment upon Israel, to have been about regional events, all of which took place in their entirety around AD 70.

The Crazy Bomb

I returned to my Bible and set out to study all the end times' subjects in the mindset of never having been taught anything about it before. Although such objectivity as this is literally impossible, I tried my best to revisit all those familiar passages with fresh eyes. Rather than starting with the book of Revelation, I began by using the words of Jesus as the starting point and foundation, from which to understand that very symbolic book. As I did, a much different version of eschatology (the study of the end times) from what I had been taught began to emerge. I knew it was time to call my cousin, Dotty. She had long ago earned the reputation in the family for being way off base. Perhaps that is short nowadays for passionate truth seeker. As I began explaining my journey with her she suddenly dropped the crazy bomb.

"Ken, I don't think you are listening to me! The 'great tribulation' and the 'Coming of the Son of Man' have both already happened in the first century around the time period of AD 70 during the destruction of the temple." At that point, I politely listened to whatever else she had to say, but secretly I was wishing the phone call would end. I had that sick feeling in my stomach that poor Dotty had gone completely off the deep end. I actually thought the sick feeling was the Holy Spirit telling me that she was so sadly wrong. I was willing to concede from my studies that the great tribulation could have happened in the first century, but to include the church's sacred 'Second Coming' in that same time period was, in my (uneducated) opinion, preposterous.

Having unintentionally triggered a truth sharing campaign in my cousin, I began receiving emails with several links to preterist view websites. Before I knew it, I was reading the historical eyewitness account by the first-century's Jewish historian, Josephus, of the unspeakably horrendous destruction of Jerusalem in AD 70. I was astonished at just how much credible historic information there is available, including several other first-century historians writing about famines in the land, a number of devastating earthquakes in that time period, all the Christians escaping Jerusalem just as they were forewarned to do by Jesus, and even during the Pax-Romana (time of great peace in the Roman Empire) there were wars and rumors of wars throughout the Roman Empire. But for me, the most shocking thing about all of this was the fact that I had sat in Christian churches for forty years and not one preacher deemed any of this amazing history important enough to tell us!

I looked up everything Dotty sent me and studied it all like a hungry animal with my Bible wide open through the entire process. I was shocked to learn that this preterist movement was so much bigger than I had thought. I bought Gary DeMar's book *Last Days Madness*, Kenneth Gentry's *The Book of Revelation Made Easy*, John L. Bray's *Matthew 24 Fulfilled*, and several other books. To my surprise, I soon discovered that if I were trying to disprove the first-century fulfillment view of the end of the age, the Bible would not be my best ally.

Mixing Oil With Water

Once I publicly conceded that the end times' doctrines I had been taught could be totally incorrect, I dislodged a huge boulder off the top of a mountain, which sent me on a journey that I was truly not prepared for. Somewhere between the "kingdom is at hand," the "age to come," and the "days of vengeance," I got lost in the mixture of oil and water. The entire New Testament seemed to contradict itself, but I knew that just could not be. So I lazily concluded that it must have been deliberately written in some riddle filled, puzzle like format that could only be properly deciphered by those who were truly willing to work hard, spend the countless hours of study, and figure it all out. Even as odd as that assessment seemed, I accepted it and decided that the pastor who has 'studied all that stuff' must know what he is talking about. Just like me, millions of other bewildered Christians had processed these oddly written passages the same way.

Over the years, my wife has repeatedly said, "I am not interested in end times stuff. I don't want to talk about it, or read about it, or study it." She has also told me several times, "Anytime the church has ever taught on that subject, I knew in my heart that what the Bible was plainly saying, and what the preacher was teaching, were two completely different things." Like my wife, at one point I stopped studying it as well. I went to work and lived my life. When I got hungry for more of God's truth I went to church and let the pastor tell me what to think, how to believe, and how to interpret the seemingly contradictive literary context on the subject of the end times.

Every now and then I would open my Bible and start reading the book of Matthew. But once again, as usual, somewhere around chapter ten my brain started perceiving the unfolding of an ancient first-century story about a soon to come judgment upon first-century Jerusalem. In verse 23 of chapter 10, Jesus tells his disciples "Truly I say to you, you shall not finish going through the cities of Israel until the Son of Man comes." Just a few pages later he tells his disciples "Truly I say to you, there are some of those who are standing here who shall not taste death until they see the Son of Man coming in his kingdom." Some will argue that he was referring to the transfiguration that took place only six to eight days later, but of course some standing there would not taste of death within the next week. I would venture to say that everyone standing there was still alive only a week later. Wouldn't you agree?

And yet our pastors were saying that all that judgment talk was referring to events still in our future, some 2000 plus years after the words were pointedly addressed to a real, live, first century audience. Huh? What Jesus seemed to be plainly saying on this subject was in such a peculiar literary conflict with what I had been taught he was saying. It seemed odd, like it didn't all add up. I have always felt that way. Like most Christians, I simply accepted that the Bible must have been intentionally written in this anomalous style that uses these ancient events to somehow prophetically paint mysterious pictures, or types, of what was to one day become our story, instead of their story. The first century people, their conversations, and their events, were to be viewed as, um, well, object lessons, if you will, like the cut-out caricatures my childhood Sunday school teacher used on a flannel illustration board.

Heart Clues About the Bible's Version of Eschatology

Jesus began his ministry with these words, "The kingdom of heaven is 'at hand'" (Matthew 4:17). John the Baptist in Matthew 3: 7-12 is seen asking the Pharisees and Sadducees "Who warned you to flee from the wrath to come?" (Matt. 3:7)

And with that 'about to come' mindset, several other verses also began falling into their logical place. "The axe is already laid at the root of the trees" (Matthew 3:10). "His winnowing fork is in his hand" (Matthew 3:12). "The age about to come" (Matthew 12:32). When someone gives the analogy of an axe having already been laid to the root of a tree, I get the sense that they are talking about something in the very near future, not an event that is 2000 years away. Likewise, when someone says a certain thing is "at hand" or "about to come," I get that same feeling of temporal nearness. And "winnowing fork is in his hand" sounds to me like someone who is just about to harvest some crops.

Then there is John the Baptist: "And if you care to accept it, he himself is Elijah, who was to come" (Matthew 11:13-14). John might not have known this about himself, but Jesus obviously did. I have heard some suggest that John the Baptist was a 'type' of Elijah (who is yet to come). It seemed like whenever people couldn't explain away plainly spoken verses in order for them to line up with their end times' doctrines, they conveniently turned them into a 'type' (no biblical support required).

In Matthew 13:40-43, Jesus is telling them that there is an unbelievably horrendous judgment coming, and if one chooses to observe literary context, it is clearly coming to the generation that Jesus was standing there speaking to. In Matthew 21:33-45 (Parable of the landowner): "They understood that he was speaking about *them*" (v. 45). So how could Jesus also be speaking about us in this verse?

Audience Relevance

When I was first shown how Jesus repeatedly said he would be coming "in his kingdom" within that first-century generation, I didn't say, "Wow, I can't believe I never saw that before!" What I said was, "That just can't be true!"

Could it be that the reason so many New Testament passages often seemed so oddly written is because our theologians had not only given them the wrong time zone, but also the wrong audience? With any passage the church deemed as end times' texts, audience relevance was never stressed as being real-time conversations taking place between the actual people Jesus was standing there talking to. It couldn't be that, because that would totally destroy the church's doctrines of a future end of the world apocalypse. Rather, we were weirdly taught to look at Jesus, as if he were some sort of master poet, holding two fingers up in a spiritually romantic, Shakespearian style, loftily chanting timeless words over the heads of the people standing there in front of him. We were essentially being told to believe, that literally all of the verses where Jesus used the word "you" when telling his original audience what they were going to see and experience, doesn't really mean they would see, or experience, any of those things? That has always bothered me.

Audience Switching

We have all heard the preacher say, "Look what Jesus is saying to us here in this verse.", or "Notice how the apostle Paul is warning us about…" All of a sudden, I realized that a most incredible thing had happened. We had literally been trained that whenever we read the New Testament to mentally remove that original first-century audience, and then insert ourselves in their place. "How absolutely insane is this!" I thought to myself. We don't even realize we are doing it, and most of us have never even thought about it. Here are just three examples of this.

In Luke 23:26-30, Jesus is seen telling the weeping women, "Daughters of Jerusalem, stop weeping for me, but weep for yourselves and for your children. For behold the days are coming when they will say, 'Blessed are the barren, and the wombs that never bore, and the breasts that never nursed.' Then they will begin to say to the mountains, 'Fall on us,' and to the hills 'Cover us.'" (Compare to Revelation 6:14-17). So was Jesus talking to them about something their children would experience? Or was he just using them as mere human storytelling stage props to talk to us about what our children may have to experience some 2000 years later? Why had this never occurred to me before?

1 Thessalonians 4:13-18: "We who are alive and remain…" Paul was talking to some folks who were mourning their dead relatives, not our dead relatives 2000 years later. What did they think about what Paul had just told them? When Paul said, "We who are alive and remain," was he not clearly referring to himself and his peers who were standing right there in front of him?

Acts 2:15-21: "This is what was spoken of through the prophet Joel: And it shall be 'in the last days…'" Peter was obviously referring to an event that was taking place then, not some event over 2000 years later. Again, I would stress that the reader be reminded that these are real, live people who are being told something that is currently happening to them in their community and in their midst. Was he not clearly stating that Acts chapter two was in the last days? Are we to believe that the 'last days' have now lasted over 2000 plus years?

Have we not mentally removed these people from their own story, and then inserted ourselves in their place? Can we really not see that we have done this? I thought to myself, "Why do we view every single book in the Old Testament in proper, historical audience relevance, and then as soon as we enter the first page of the New Testament we switch the off button on audience relevance? What if the key to fully understanding biblical eschatology is simply to believe that the New Testament is an actual true story that unfolded in history to the very audience it is clearly telling us it was unfolding for?" Is this something our hearts have always been trying to tell us?

Was Jesus Using People?

Perhaps it is not the Bible that has confused man, but man who has confused the Bible. According to most of today's end times' preachers, Jesus was running around in that first century telling people that something was going to happen to them, that didn't happen to them and wouldn't happen to them. These same 'Jesus is coming soon' folks would also have us believe that Jesus basically *used* the people of that first-century generation merely as some sort of illustration tools or human storytelling stage props, if you will, and that he was not really talking to (or about) them or what they would experience, but to (and about) us, in a time setting some 2000 plus years later. That would directly imply that Jesus and the apostles either premeditatedly lied directly to their faces, or had absolutely no idea what they were talking about. That concept has always been difficult for me to believe. At this point, I knew that I was starting to ask the right questions.

The What and When Questions

In Matthew chapter 24, Jesus is answering the disciples' questions. His answer starts at verse 4 and goes all the way up through verse 34 (verse 34 clearly answering the when part of their question). The disciples were pointing out the temple buildings to Jesus, and he said to them (about the temple buildings), "Do you not see all these things? Truly I say to you, not one stone here shall be left upon another, which will not be torn down." It is also imperative for us to realize that Matthew chapter 24 is a continuation of the conversation in chapter 23 with the Scribes and Pharisees. Please take note of 23:38: "Behold, your house (the temple) is being left to you desolate!" Only three verses later, Jesus is telling the disciples how that very house/temple will be completely destroyed. The disciples are shocked, and ask a time-based question: "Tell us, when will these things be, and what will be the sign of your coming and of the end of the age." Unfortunately, the King James version incorrectly uses the word "world" instead of "age," which all the newer versions have long since corrected.

Matthew 24:34 "Truly I say to you (his disciples), this generation will not pass away until all these things take place." I thought to myself, "Wouldn't all these things have to include the destruction of the temple in Matthew 24:2?" It was becoming increasingly obvious to me at this point, that Jesus was not talking to cardboard cutout story props that resemble people. He was standing there looking into the eyes of real, live people, telling them all these things.

Surrounded by Armies

Luke 21:20 "But when you (disciples) see Jerusalem surrounded by armies, then recognize that her desolation is at hand." This actually happened in 66 AD, just thirty seven years later (in their generation), just as Jesus had foretold it would in Matthew 24:2. So not only would they see this event, but so would "those who pierced Him," for they would also still be alive.

In Luke 21:22, Jesus added, "Because these are the days of vengeance, in order that all things which are written may be fulfilled." "These days" clearly means the days when armies would be seen (by his disciples) surrounding Jerusalem. But according to the end times' "experts," it should have said "some things," not "all things."

Thinking of all these things as distant, future, worldwide calamities was not only looking more and more manufactured, but totally illogical and completely out of literary context.

Ancient, Regional Events, or Future Global Apocalypse?

In Luke 19:43-44, the army uses ancient Roman military tactics of taking a city (they build siege mounds around the city). Why would a twenty-first century mechanized military with high-tech missiles, fighter jets, and pinpoint accuracy, smart bombs build an embankment or siege mound? Such a military operation is obviously describing ancient warfare that would enable the Romans to eventually penetrate the high city walls. The Pharisaical Sabbath laws are still in effect (Mt. 24:20). Why would there be a twenty-first century concern about the Sabbath laws when such laws have been out of civil use for 2000 years? The disciples are to be persecuted by synagogues and brought before kings (Mk. 13:9). What twenty-first century synagogues will stand in judgment over believers? The Christians are to flee Judea and go to the mountains (Mt. 24:16). The people are dwelling in flat-roofed houses. (Mt. 24:17). This great tribulation obviously has reference to the Jews living in Palestine in the first century. Where are the flat roofs that people must not return to? Who in Tokyo or Sydney or Minneapolis will be able to see the abomination of desolation? How can we even apply these passages to a twenty-first century Jerusalem, let alone somewhere else on the planet?

What was I to do? The easy, more popular path would be to just ignore all this audience-relevant, in-context information. Do I just say, "So what if Jesus taught something different than what my church teaches"? Is that really how I am going to process all these things? Am I actually that loyal to my indoctrination that not even the words of Jesus can change it?

Those Who Are in Judea

Luke 21:21 "Then let those who are in Judea flee to the mountains." What does history have to say about this?

The early Christian (first-century) scholar Eusebius wrote:

> The whole body, however, of the church at Jerusalem, having been commanded by a divine revelation, given to men of approved piety there before the war, removed from the city, and dwelt at a certain town beyond the Jordan, called Pella.

Epiphanes also attested to the Christian escape:

> It is very remarkable that not a single Christian perished in the destruction of Jerusalem, though there were many there when Cestius Gallus invested the city; and, had he persevered in the siege, he would soon have rendered himself master of it; but, when he unexpectedly and unaccountably raised the siege, the Christians took that opportunity to escape. ... [As] Vespasian was approaching with his army, all who believed in Christ left Jerusalem and fled to Pella, and other places beyond the river Jordan; and so they all marvelously escaped the general shipwreck of their country: not one of them perished.

The Actual Historical Account of the Destruction of the Temple in AD 70

Our only firsthand account of the Roman assault on the Temple comes from the Jewish historian Josephus Flavius. In the year AD 66, the Jews of Judea rebelled against their Roman masters. In response, the Emperor Nero dispatched an army under the generalship of Vespasian to restore order. By the year 68, resistance in the northern part of the province had been eradicated and the Romans turned their full attention to the subjugation of Jerusalem. That same year, the Emperor Nero died by his own hand, creating a power vacuum in Rome. In the resultant chaos, Vespasian was declared Emperor and returned to the Imperial City. It fell to his son, Titus, to lead the remaining army in the assault on Jerusalem.

The Roman legions surrounded the city and began to slowly squeeze the life out of the Jewish stronghold. By the year 70, the attackers had breached Jerusalem's outer walls and began a systematic ransacking of the city. The assault culminated in the burning and destruction of the Temple that served as the center of Judaism.

In victory, the Romans slaughtered thousands. Of those spared from death: thousands were enslaved and sent to toil in the mines of Egypt; others were dispersed to arenas throughout the Empire to be butchered for the amusement of the public. The Temple's sacred relics were taken to Rome where they were displayed in celebration of the victory. Here is that astonishing eyewitness written history:

> The rebels shortly after attacked the Romans again, and a clash followed between the guards of the sanctuary and the troops who were putting out the fire inside the inner court; the latter routed the Jews and followed in hot pursuit right up to the Temple itself. Then one of the soldiers, without awaiting any orders and with no dread of so momentous a deed, but urged on by some supernatural force, snatched a blazing piece of wood and, climbing on another soldier's back, hurled the flaming brand through a low golden window that gave access, on the north side, to the rooms that surrounded the sanctuary. As the flames shot up, the Jews let out a shout of dismay that matched the tragedy; they flocked to the rescue, with no thought of sparing their lives or husbanding their strength; for the sacred structure that they had constantly guarded with such devotion was vanishing before their very eyes.
>
> No exhortation or threat could now restrain the impetuosity of the legions; for passion was in supreme command. Crowded together around the entrances, many were trampled down by their companions; others, stumbling on the smoldering and smoked-filled ruins of the porticoes, died as miserably as the defeated. As they drew closer to the Temple, they pretended not even to hear Caesar's orders, but urged the men in front to throw in more firebrands. The rebels were powerless to help; carnage and flight spread throughout.
>
> Most of the slain were peaceful citizens, weak and unarmed, and they were butchered where they were caught. The heap of corpses mounted higher and higher about the altar; a stream of blood flowed down the Temple's steps, and the bodies of those slain at the top slipped to the bottom.

When Caesar failed to restrain the fury of his frenzied soldiers, and the fire could not be checked, he entered the building with his generals and looked at the holy place of the sanctuary and all its furnishings, which exceeded by far the accounts current in foreign lands and fully justified their splendid repute in our own.

As the flames had not yet penetrated to the inner sanctum, but were consuming the chambers that surrounded the sanctuary, Titus assumed correctly that there was still time to save the structure; he ran out and by personal appeals he endeavored to persuade his men to put out the fire, instructing Liberalius, a centurion of his bodyguard of lancers, to club any of the men who disobeyed his orders. But their respect for Caesar and their fear of the centurion's staff who was trying to check them were overpowered by their rage, their detestation of the Jews, and an utterly uncontrolled lust for battle.

Most of them were spurred on, moreover, by the expectation of loot, convinced that the interior was full of money and dazzled by observing that everything around them was made of gold. But they were forestalled by one of those who had entered into the building, and who, when Caesar dashed out to restrain the troops, pushed a firebrand, in the darkness, into the hinges of the gate. Then, when the flames suddenly shot up from the interior, Caesar and his generals withdrew, and no one was left to prevent those outside from kindling the blaze. Thus, in defiance of Caesar's wishes, the Temple was set on fire.

While the Temple was ablaze, the attackers plundered it, and countless people who were caught by them were slaughtered. There was no pity for age and no regard was accorded rank; children and old men, laymen and priests, alike were butchered; every class was pursued and crushed in the grip of war, whether they cried out for mercy or offered resistance.

Through the roar of the flames streaming far and wide, the groans of the falling victims were heard; such was the height of the hill and the magnitude of the blazing pile that the entire city seemed to be ablaze; and the noise -- nothing more deafening and frightening could be imagined.

There were the war cries of the Roman legions as they swept onwards en masse, the yells of the rebels encircled by fire and sword, the panic of the people who, cut off above, fled into the arms of the enemy, and their shrieks as they met their fate. The cries on the hill blended with those of the multitudes in the city below; and now many people who were exhausted and tongue-tied as a result of hunger, when they beheld the Temple on fire, found strength once more to lament and wail. Peraea and the surrounding hills, added their echoes to the deafening din. But more horrifying than the din were the sufferings.

The Temple Mount, everywhere enveloped in flames, seemed to be boiling over from its base; yet the blood seemed more abundant than the flames and the numbers of the slain greater than those of the slayers. The soldiers climbed over heaps of bodies as they chased the fugitives."

Josephus said, "It was then common to see cities filled with dead bodies, still lying unburied, and those old men mixed with infants all dead and scattered about together." Josephus reports that above 600,000 corpses of those that perished in the siege of Jerusalem were cast out of the city gates of Jerusalem into the lake of fire known as Gehenna."

Gehenna was the garbage dump outside of Jerusalem in the valley of Hinnom where bodies are burned and eaten by worms and maggots. This is the 'hell-fire' Jesus warned apostate Jews about in all of the synoptic gospels.

References: Josephus' account appears in: Cornfield, Gaalya ed., Josephus, The Jewish War (1982); Duruy, Victor, History of Rome vol. V (1883).

After Jerusalem was destroyed, Josephus writes that Titus "gave orders that they should now demolish the whole city and temple," except three towers, which he reserved standing. But for the rest of the wall, it was laid so completely even with the ground by those who "dug it up from the foundation," that there was nothing left to make those believe who came hither that it had ever been inhabited." Maimonides, a Jewish writer, has also recorded that "Terentius Rufus, an officer in the army of Titus, with a plowshare tore up the foundations of the temple, that the prophecy might be fulfilled, 'Zion shall be plowed as a field,'" (Micah 3:12)

This Generation

My questions continued. How is it that theologians have decided that all throughout the New Testament, the term "this generation" DOES mean the first-century generation EXCEPT for Matthew 23:36, Matthew 24:34, Mark 13:30, and Luke 21:32? Many scholars are actually at a loss as to why Jesus failed to keep his promise. But is that even possible?

Shocking Statement by C.S. Lewis

C.S. Lewis, admired by many Christians for his great, inspirational writings, said this:

> Christianity is the story of how the rightful king has landed, you might say landed in disguise, and is calling us all to take part in a great campaign of sabotage.

The following quotation is from his sermon, "The World's Last Night."

> The apocalyptic beliefs of the first Christians have been proved to be false. It is clear from the New Testament that they all expected the Second Coming in their own lifetime. And, worse still, they had a reason, and one which you will find very embarrassing. Their Master had told them so. He shared, and indeed created their delusion. He said in so many words, "this generation shall not pass till all these things be done." And he was wrong. He clearly knew no more about the end of the world than anyone else. This is certainly the most embarrassing verse in the Bible.

C.S. Lewis is to be commended, I think, for being theologically honest enough to admit the obvious New Testament's billboard-like display of how Jesus clearly taught a first-century coming, and also how the Christians in that century clearly expected that return in their lifetimes. But what he obviously failed to recognize is that it was the end of the (Mosaic) age, not the end of the world that Jesus was talking about. If we are brave enough to objectively rethink this subject, we will find that Jesus was talking about the time of the end of an age and an old covenant, not the end of time.

Expectancy of This 'Coming' Throughout the Entire New Testament

These are all both vivid and powerful displays of how that first-century generation expected what Jesus called his "coming" during their lifetimes.

> "If I want him (John) to remain until I come, what is that to you?" (John 21:22).

> "…but this is what was spoken of through the prophet Joel: And it shall be in the last days,…" (Acts 2:16).

> "He has fixed a day in which He is to judge the world in righteousness" (Acts 17:31).

> "But as he was discussing righteousness, self-control and the judgment to come…" (Acts 24:25).

> "You know what hour it is, how it is full time now for you to wake from sleep. For salvation is nearer to us now than when we first believed; the night is far gone, the day is at hand" (Romans 13:11-12).

> "The God of peace will soon crush Satan under your feet" (Romans 16:20).

> "Brethren, the appointed time has grown very short; from now on, let those who have wives live as though they had none, and those who mourn as though they were not mourning, and those who rejoice as though they were not rejoicing, and those who buy as though they had no goods, and those who deal with the world as though they had no dealings with it. For the form of this world is passing away" (1 Corinthians 7:29-31).

"On us the ends of the ages have come" (1 Corinthians 10:11).

"The Lord is at hand" (Philippians 4:5).

"The coming of the Lord is at hand. ... Behold, the Judge is standing at the door" (James 5:8-9).

"The end of all things is at hand" (1 Peter 4:7).

"It is the last hour ... we know that it is the last hour" (1 John 2:18).

(Heb. 9:8-10. See also Gal. 4:19; Eph. 2:21-22; 3:17; 4:13).

"The world is passing away, and its desires" (1 John 2:17).

"But you, beloved, ought to remember the words that were spoken beforehand by the apostles of our Lord Jesus Christ, that they were saying to you, 'In the last time there shall be mockers, following after their own ungodly lusts.' These are the ones who cause divisions." (Jude 1:17-19).

"Not only in this age, but also in the one to come" (Ephesians 1:21).

"Things which are a shadow of what is to come" (Colossians 2:16-17).

"May your spirit and soul and body be preserved complete, without blame at the coming of our Lord Jesus Christ" (1 Thessalonians. 5:23).

"Godliness ... holds promise for the present life and that which is to come" (1 Timothy 4:8).

"I charge you ... that you keep the commandment without stain or reproach until the appearing of our Lord Jesus Christ" (1 Timothy 6:14).

"In the last days difficult times will come. For men will be lovers of self ... Avoid these men. For of these are those who enter into households and captivate weak women ... These also oppose the truth ... But they will not make further progress; for their folly will be obvious to all." (2 Timothy 3:1-9).

"I solemnly charge you in the presence of God and of Christ Jesus, who is about to judge the living and the dead." (2 Timothy 4:1).

"God, after He spoke long ago to the fathers in the prophets in many portions and in many ways, in these last days has spoken to us in His Son" (Hebrews 1:1-2).

"He did not subject to angels the world to come" (Hebrews 2:5).

"When He said, 'A new covenant,' He has made the first obsolete. But whatever is becoming obsolete and growing old is ready to disappear" (Hebrews 8:13).

"But when Christ appeared as a high priest of the good things about to come." (Hebrews 9:11).

"Now once at the consummation of the ages He has been manifested to put away sin" (Hebrews 9:26).

"For the Law, since it has only a shadow of the good things to come." (Hebrews 10:1).

"As you see the Day drawing near" (Hebrews 10:25).

"The fury of a fire which is about to consume the adversaries" (Hebrews 10:27).

"For yet in a very little while, He who is coming will come, and will not delay" (Hebrews 10:37).

"For here we do not have a lasting city, but we are seeking the one that is to come" (Hebrews 13:14).

"Come now, you rich, weep and howl for your miseries which are coming upon you. ... It is in the last days that you have stored up your treasure!" (James 5:1, 3).

"Be patient, therefore, brethren, until the coming of the Lord" (James 5:7).

"You too be patient; strengthen your hearts, for the coming of the Lord is at hand" (James 5:8).

"Salvation ready to be revealed in the last time" (1 Peter 1:5).

"They shall give account to Him who is ready to judge the living and the dead" (1 Peter 4:5).

"The end of all things is at hand; therefore, be of sound judgment and sober spirit for the purpose of prayer" (1 Peter 4:7).

"For it is time for judgment to begin with the household of God" (1 Peter 4:17).

"As your fellow elder and witness of the sufferings of Christ, and a partaker also of the glory that is to be revealed" (1 Peter 5:1).

"In the last days mockers will come. ... For this they willingly are ignorant of..." (1 Peter 3:3, 5).

"But the day of the Lord will come like a thief, in which the heavens will pass away with a roar and the elements will be destroyed with intense heat, and the earth and its works will be burned up. Since all these things are to be destroyed in this way, what sort of people ought you to be in holy conduct and godliness, looking for and hastening the coming of the day of God" (2 Pet. 3:10-12).

"It is the last hour" (1 John 2:18).

"Even now many antichrists have arisen; from this we *know* that it is the last hour" (1 John 2:18. See also Matt. 24:23-34).

"This is that of the antichrist, of which you have heard that it is coming, and now it is already in the world" (1 John 4:3. See also 2 Thessalonians 2:7).

The "judgment to come" was obviously referring to Matthew 24:2 and Luke 21:20-22. A new age was about to begin, and they knew that the "ends of the ages" was coming in their generation. They clearly believed that the "coming of the Lord" (whatever that meant) was "at hand". They said that "The end of all things is at hand". But the end of what things? The "world" that was about to pass away was the old Judaic religion and covenant, not the planet earth. They knew that they were "in the last days", and said so with boldness. They could see this day drawing near. How is it that we have taken their (first-century) story and made it our (twenty-first century) story?

So, were all these people wrong? The end times 'experts' actually think they were. We can clearly see what the Bible says, but that's not what we've been told it says, is it?

Jerusalem Was Destroyed in AD 70?

I didn't know that Roman armies, carrying the bold ensigns of an eagle, surrounded Jerusalem between AD 66 and 68 exactly as Jesus said they would. Did you know that? My pastors never told me that. And I didn't know that the temple in Jerusalem was destroyed (and then completely and methodically dismantled right down to its foundation) from the orders of a Roman madman (Nero Caesar) of whom throughout the entire region had the well-known nickname, "the Beast." Nero was the sixth king that gave the order for Jerusalem to be destroyed. The order of the Roman emperors was as follows:

1. Julius Caesar
2. Augustus
3. Tiberius
4. Gaius (Caligula)
5. Claudius
6. Nero (AD 54-68). The Beast (which most, if not all, scholars agree represents Rome) was ruled by its sixth head (head = king), which was already in existence in John's day.

Of the seven heads (kings), only one was left by AD 95. Rome was long past its seventh Caesar. A second century manuscript of Revelation says it was written when Nero was Caesar (AD 68). When the disciples (who would have still been alive then) "saw the armies surrounding Jerusalem," would they not have remembered the conversation Jesus had with them in Luke 21:20? The same goes for when they saw the temple (that was still standing in Revelation 11:1-2) being destroyed in Jerusalem, "the great city where our Lord was crucified."

100-Pound Catapulted Boulders?

I also didn't know that first century history (*War with the Jews* by Flavius Josephus) eloquently documented the Roman army hurling 100-pound boulders at the city of Jerusalem, nor just how horrendous that was in real life for the recipients of those 'hailstones' until I actually read the documented history on the subject (Rev. 16:21). I had never been shown the historical documentation of how the Romans eventually had to paint those (white) 100-pound boulders black so the Jews could no longer see them coming to run out of their path. No wonder they called them 'hailstones.'

Here is an excerpt from that historic document:

> Now the stones that were cast were of the weight of a talent, and were carried two furlongs and further. The blow they gave was no way to be sustained, not only by those that stood first in the way, but by those that were beyond them for a great space. As for the Jews, they at first watched the coming of the stone, for it was of a white color, and could therefore not only be perceived by the great noise it made, but could be seen also before it came by its brightness; accordingly the watchmen that sat upon the towers gave them notice when the engine was let go, and the stone came from it, and cried out aloud, in their own country language, THE STONE COMETH so those that were in its way stood off, and threw themselves down upon the ground; by which means, and by their thus

guarding themselves, the stone fell down and did them no harm. But the Romans contrived how to prevent that by blacking the stone, who then could aim at them with success, when the stone was not discerned beforehand, as it had been till then; and so they destroyed many of them at one blow.

Seven Churches. Real, First-Century Churches?

I didn't know that the "seven churches" in the book of Revelation were actually real, first-century churches full of harshly persecuted Christians. Nor did I know that the order in which they are listed in Revelation was in the same order of a well-known, first-century Roman mail delivery route to all of those towns over on the mainland. Another amazing historical fact is that the only time there were only seven churches in Asia was in the early 60s.

I had never even stopped for a minute to examine for myself the very theme of this letter called Revelation. For instance, in the very first verse of the first chapter, John plainly states who his actual audience is (his bondservants), and then proceeds to tell them that his letter is about things "which must shortly take place" for them. In Revelation 1:3, John is saying that the very reason his bondservants are to "heed the things which are written in it" is because "the time is near." Why would John boldly tell those people that the very purpose of his letter was about things that are very near for them, if they absolutely were not? I had never been challenged by the church to even ask that question.

John's letter to those real people, in those real churches, was sent to minister to them, being a "fellow partaker in the tribulation," to give them spiritual instruction, encouragement, and hope. John is writing to seven actual churches in horrendous circumstances. He expected them to decipher and comprehend the very symbolic and metaphorical things he was writing to them. I, myself, had never even thought about that, nor the possibility of what seems so confusing to our generation, being quite easy for that culture to decipher.

Here Is a Big Part of What Was Written to Those Fellow Partakers:

"Things which must shortly take place" (Revelation 1:1).

"The hour of trial ... is about to come upon the whole world" (3:10).

"Behold, I come quickly!" (3:11).

"Things which must shortly take place" (22:6).

"Behold, I am coming quickly!" (22:7).

"Do not seal up the words of the prophecy of this book, for the time is near" (22:10).

"Behold, I am coming quickly" (22:12).

"Surely I am coming quickly" (22:20). εγγυς, engus means, at hand, near.

"The time is near" (1:3).

"The time is at hand" (22:10). μελλει, mello, mellei means, about to, on the point or verge of.

"Write ... the things that are about to take place" (1:19).

Interestingly, the opening and closing statements of the book of Revelation were talking about the same opening and closing statements of the Olivet discourse by Jesus himself:

"Things which must shortly take place" (Rev 1:1). "For the time is near" (1:3).

"Things which must shortly take place" (22:6). "For the time is near" (22:10).

"Truly I say to you, all these things shall come upon this generation" (Matt. 23:36).

"Truly I say to you, this generation will not pass away until all these things (in v. 2-34) take place" (Matt. 24:34).

Was God just using those poor people for a story that was not even about them? Would it not in fact be a very sick joke, if John was just using those peoples' dire situation and their desperate hope, as human storytelling props for some other future generation? Can we not see just how utterly insane that sounds? Have we not literally stolen someone else's ancient story? Isn't this just another example where we have been trained to mentally remove the original audience and then carelessly insert ourselves in their place? It doesn't make logical sense, and my heart has always known it.

To Seal Up, Or Not To Seal Up?

The time (500 years) in the book of Daniel was not near (Dan. 12:4), but the time in Rev 22:10 was near. If Revelation was not to be sealed because the "time is near," but Daniel was to be sealed because it was for "many days" and the "time of the end" (Daniel 10:14, 12:4, 9), then "many days" are 500 years. If that is true, how can "at hand" or "the time is near" be over 2000 years? Not only have we never asked ourselves that question, but we have never even thought about this possible literary inconsistency of discrepancy in the meaning of time.

As It Was in the Days of Noah?

I didn't know that the words "one will be taken and one will be left" in Matthew 24:37-39 (which is to mirror the days of Noah) is actually saying that the one left is the one spared, otherwise it would not be "as it was in the days of Noah," because the flood came, and took them all away; so shall also the coming of the Son of man be. But it doesn't end there: "And they answered and said unto Him, where, Lord? And he (Jesus) said unto them, wheresoever the body is, thither will the eagles be gathered together." Where? Where the carcass is! Where the dead body is! Where the place of death and destruction is.

The idea that Matthew 24 is talking about taking away the Christians in a rapture is not at all the case. The biblical narrative shows that the true followers are left behind after destruction takes the wicked out. Where? In Jerusalem. When? In AD 70, at the destruction of the Temple. The Romans were like an eagle, and the ensign of their armies was an eagle, and every legion bore the eagle as its standard. When we are honest enough to match the history with the plainly written literary context of the biblical account, it all comes together exactly as it was always meant to come together. And it is not a riddle, but simply a true story that actually happened a long, long time ago.

Wars and Rumors of Wars in the First Century?

I didn't know that the well-known, first-century, Jewish historian, Josephus, wrote that "Roman civil wars were so common" in the Roman Empire that there was "no need to write about them in great detail." He recorded that more than 50,000 Jews were killed at Seleucia. The Annuls of Tacitus (AD 14 - 68) talks about the tumult of that period, speaking of skirmishes, battles, and wars in dozens of places throughout the reach of the Roman Empire.

Famines in the Land in the First Century?

I had never connected the dots of the horrendous famines in the land in the first century being those of the "last days". Great famines in the land are obvious throughout the New Testament (Acts 11:27-29; 1 Cor. 16:1-5; Rom. 15:25-28). Many secular historians of that time period also wrote of several horrific famines.

Earthquakes in Different Places in the First Century?

I didn't know that there were many catastrophic earthquakes in the first century. By the way, Jesus never once said anything about an increase in their number, as end times' preachers often do for some odd reason. Earthquakes are mentioned prior to the destruction of Jerusalem in AD 70, one at the crucifixion, at the resurrection, and another in Acts 16:26 that shook the foundations of a prison. Secular historians of that same time period record many earthquakes in Crete, Smyrna, Militus, Chios, Samos, Laodicea, Hierapolis, Calosse, Campania, Rome, and Judea. Josephus describes an earthquake in Judea of such devastation "that the constitution of the universe was confounded for the destruction of men."

The Great Tribulation in the First Century?

The great tribulation of the saints is clearly documented all throughout the New Testament and the book of Revelation, and also in the book of Acts (4:1-22; 5:17-40; 8:1-3; 12:1-9; 14:19-20; 16:22-23; 22:30). The tribulation was all about the first-century Jews and for those in Judea (Matt. 24:16; Luke 21:20-24). It was not about some future twenty-first century global event. The seven-year period of tribulation spoken of in the Book of Daniel is clearly shown to be the seven years between AD 63 and AD 70. In year AD 63, the Jews revolted against Rome, which gave way to an unspeakably horrific seven-year period in which millions of Jews were killed, ending with the complete destruction and utter desolation of their temple and the city of Jerusalem in AD 70.

End Times False Prophets in the First Century "Last Days"?

The Apostle Peter writes, "False prophets also arose among the people, just as there will also be false teachers among you, who will secretly introduce destructive heresies." (2 Peter 2:1, 2:2-3; 2 Cor. 11:13; Acts 13:6; 2 Tim. 2:16-17; Acts 20:29-30; I Tim 4:1; 2 Tim. 3:13; I John 4:1; 2 John 7; I John 2:18).

End of the Age in the First Century?

I didn't know that the end of the age refers to the end of the old covenant redemptive system with its attendant sacrifices and rituals, which were designed to be temporary symbols. The end of the age refers to the termination of the exclusive Jewish entitlement to the covenant promises, and the inclusion of the Gentiles into the blessing of the covenant and the privileges of the kingdom (Matt. 21:41, 43; 22:10; John 1:21, 2:13-22; Heb. 8:2; John 1:14; Heb. 2:17, 3:1, 5:1-10, 7:26-28; Eph. 2:11-22; Heb. 10:4, 9:1-28). In short, this is all someone else's ancient story, not ours.

New Jerusalem Not an Actual City?

I had heard preachers talking romantically about the New Jerusalem being a large golden city that will one day come down from heaven and land in Jerusalem. What they did not tell me is that according to the measurements in Revelation, this golden city would be 1,500 miles cubed. If that were an actual Borg-like object coming down to earth from outer space, it would completely cover the entire Middle East including all of Egypt, Turkey, Iraq, Syria, Jordan, Israel, Saudi Arabia, a huge section of the Mediterranean Sea, and several parts of other neighboring countries. For a more familiar mental picture, it is 1,500 miles from Seattle to Minneapolis, not to mention extending 1,200 miles out beyond the International Space Station. So, basically, I was being asked to believe that a colossal cubed city almost as large as our MOON will one day come down from outer space and completely cover the entire Middle East, all without affecting the ocean, gravity, or the orbital mechanics of our planet.

I now realize of course that the New Jerusalem is not a literal 1,500-mile cubed city, but rather a metaphorically symbolic picture of the Bride of Christ (please refer to Hebrews 12:22 or Revelation 21:9). Hence, "I will show you the Bride." In my honest opinion, it is nothing short of insane what theologians have constructed from those ancient metaphorical writings.

If We Are Already in the Kingdom, Then Why Is There So Much Sin in the World?

In the last chapter of Revelation, John writes that those who believe (while in this physical life) enter in at the gate, and those who don't are outside the gate, spiritually, and that they will always be with us, in this part of our life. So, if the last chapter of Revelation is about some perfect physical kingdom being here, then who are the dogs and sorcerers and immoral persons and murderers and idolaters and whosoever loveth and maketh a lie? What are they doing in a perfect, magical kingdom? And, why is there the need for a "tree" (Revelation 22.2), of which its leaves are for the "healing of the nations," in a Utopian physical paradise with no tears, pain, or death?

What About the Gospel Being Preached in the Whole World?

> "This gospel of the kingdom shall be preached in the whole world as a testimony to all the nations, and then the end will come" (Matt. 24:14).

"The whole world," in context, is referring to that particular region: "The gospel that you have heard, which was proclaimed in all creation under heaven, and of which I, Paul, was made a minister." (Col. 1:23). Also, in Colossians 1:6 Paul talked about how the gospel was "constantly bearing fruit and increasing in all the world [kosmos]," "to all nations" (16:26), and "devout men, from every nation under heaven" (Rom. 16:25-27; Acts 11:28, Acts 2:5). Paul states in AD 55 that "the word of Christ" has already gone [aorist verb: past tense] "to the ends of the earth [oikumene]" (Rom. 10:18). One should also note the words "all the world" in the census ordered by Caesar Augustus (Luke 2:1-3). It is quite obvious that "the whole world" meant either the Roman Empire or the scope of that particular region, not the entire planet.

But Wasn't the Book of Revelation Written After AD 70?

Critics of the older preterist view often point out that the Book of Revelation was written sometime between AD 95-96, and therefore it could not have prophesied events taking place in AD 63-70. Even though most leading Bible translations claim the late date, the truth is there is no solid evidence to suggest that the Book of Revelation was written that late in the first century. On the contrary, the evidence for Revelation being written before 63 is beyond overwhelming. My first draft of this section was a three-page list of the unavoidable historical and literary facts that make the late date impossible. For those who wish to be able to say they have done their honest due diligence on this subject, I highly recommend the book *Before Jerusalem Fell: Dating the Book of Revelation* by Kenneth L. Gentry.

The Kingdom: a Physical Paradise or Spiritual Reality?

"Before long, the world will not see me anymore, but you will see me. Because I live, you also will live" (John 14:19). How can Jesus' kingdom be physical when Jesus clearly rejected a physical kingdom? Why did Jesus leave earth after his resurrection, if he really wanted to establish an earthly physical kingdom here? Why didn't He just stay here? How can Jesus' kingdom be set up in earthly Jerusalem, when Jesus himself said the hour was coming when worshiping God would not be in Jerusalem (John 4:21)? And why would Jesus' kingdom be set up in earthly Jerusalem, when Jesus condemned their city several times (Matt. 21-25)? Also, Paul said earthly Jerusalem was bondage and the old covenant (Gal. 4:24-25). How can Jesus› kingdom have not yet come, when John the Baptist, Jesus himself, and the apostles all declared the "kingdom of God is at hand" (Matt. 3:2, 4:17, 10:7)? How can everyone physically see Jesus' kingdom when Jesus himself said it comes not with observation (Luke 17:20)? And lastly, how can Jesus' kingdom be worldly, earthly, or physical, when Jesus himself said, "My kingdom is not of this world" (John 18:36)?

Coming on the Clouds

So much of the language used in the gospels and Revelation about Jesus coming on the clouds is the same judgment imagery language used throughout the Old Testament. The coming on the clouds we read about in the gospels is from Old Testament portrayals of God descending from heaven and coming in power to execute judgment on ancient wicked nations and cities, and in deliverance of His people. These 'judgments' were acts of God described in figurative language. Don K. Preston has written some great articles on this subject (Google it). A pattern of covenantal language is also being repeatedly used, like "Heaven and Earth passing away," etc. So did Jesus actually come down in the clouds over Jerusalem in AD 70? Was this coming more of a spiritual event, or a prophetically historical event? In an ancient Middle Eastern culture where priests and prophets where a part of the judicial branch of government, is it even a possibility that this entire saga was simply the religious sect's take on current, historical events? The questions we should be asking are: When did Jesus say this 'coming' would take place? Who did he say it directly to? What were the signs he told them they would see? And did those signs take place during the lifetimes of his original audience? The answer, of course, is, yes.

I was also beginning to realize what my heart had suspected for some time: We (incorrectly) assume that by simply studying the Hebrew and Greek we can achieve a full comprehension of those ancient documents, but is such hermeneutical idealism really true? Many of those ancient texts are bewildering to us here in the twenty-first century, but not to those in the first-century. They fully understood all the folklore, legends, mysticism, spiritualism, poetic speech, mythology, figures-of-speech, metaphors, regional slang, and nomadic wording. Their language, unknown to us, was richly seasoned with the cultures and religions of their time (including ancient Roman, Greek, Asian, and certainly Egyptian influences, not to mention astrology). None of these things I just mentioned were even a second thought for them. The same is true for us; how the works of Shakespeare, first and second-world-war military terms, judicial terms, sayings from romantic literature, and a host of other influences our language has, that would be completely misunderstood by some far-removed Chinese culture 2,000 years from now.

It is not the words of Jesus and the apostles concerning the timing of the end of the age, that need to somehow awkwardly fit into our eschatology, but our (awkward) eschatology that needs to fit into what Jesus and the apostles said concerning the timing of all these things. The fact that this is not the exegetical method of how we have approached this study speaks volumes of how far the church has yet to come.

Trying to Disprove the Words of Jesus.

In order for us to maintain a futurist position of eschatology, we must work very hard and very creatively, to explain away the very clearly-spoken, plainly-recorded words of Jesus. He stood there looking in the eyes of people - telling them what they would see and experience. Not to mention John on the Island of Patmos doing the same thing... pointedly saying who his audience and recipients were. This... "coming" or "return" was probably not what we (or others) thought it was. What we do know is what generation Jesus said it would be happening to. That is more than abundantly clear. And that is what we must creatively explain away if we are to continue promoting a future return. Jesus either lied to those people, used them as theatrical story-telling stage props, or He was telling them the truth. Those who still insist on a future return of Jesus must base their entire foundation for their position on the idea that Jesus couldn't have possibly meant what he clearly and plainly said. And rather than making what Jesus said their foundation and starting point, they actually (unknowingly) set out to disprove what he said. I know, because I did the exact same thing, and for years.

What Does It All Mean? What Does It Change?

Preachers can do all sorts of creative exegetical dance moves, but they cannot make biblical references such as "at hand," or "is about to come," or "this generation," or "things which must shortly take place" mean 2000 years later. It blatantly contradicts the very theme and literary context, of the plainly laid-out, audience relevant story itself.

Once I really came to grips with the Bible's version of the end of the age and the coming of the Son of Man, my entire Christian belief system started changing. It had to. The first instinct for those of us who have gone through this awkward, corrective process, is that we want all of our 800 questions completely satisfied within the next twenty minutes. And for some, if they can only get 795 of them answered, they'll take the five unanswered ones and default back to the church's official (futurist) position. I am continually shocked by this seemingly careless reaction. I had to ask myself if I too was going to take that non-confrontational route. Do I hang on tight to the four or five verses that could still be used to support what I had been taught, or will I be intellectually honest with myself about the bulk and exegetical weight of the Bible's clearly written story of a first-century event having taken place in its entirety? The third (popular) choice is to just not think or talk about it anymore and hope it all just goes away.

I began to realize that this doesn't just change a few things about the timing of past events. It changes everything! It changes our understanding of biblical terms and concepts like judgment, wrath, and so many other doctrines that are also directly attached to this first-century story. Even though all those ancient passages contain great amounts of wisdom and valuable spiritual principles, I was beginning to realize that much of the context was not only first-century specific, but ancient Judaism specific. In a nutshell, this is all about someone else's ancient Middle Eastern religion. We were never the intended recipients or the audience of that letter called Revelation, or any other 'last days' texts throughout the New Testament. Since the great tribulation, the end of the age, and the coming of the Son of man (whatever that symbolized) already happened in the first century, those things are not going to happen *again* in our future. What was already completely fulfilled does not get fulfilled again.

Several other things were also included in that first-century event, like the sword that Jesus was bringing instead of peace, the clearing of His threshing floor, the parable of the tares, and parables of the Landowner and the Marriage feast, and the Seven Woes in Matthew chapter 23. When Jesus said "Woe to you, Bethsaida and Capernaum," he did not (actually) mean Boston and Cleveland.

Since all that wrath talk in the gospels was clearly referring to a first-century war between Rome and Jerusalem, then it cannot also be about some sort of dark, twisted science fiction fantasy courtroom in the sky after we die, where we will all one day find ourselves on trial for being human. The 'sheep and the goats' cannot be referring to both a first-century judgment upon Jerusalem, and the difference between modern-day Christians and non-Christians. And since the "days of vengeance" were clearly referring to the days when the disciples would see armies surrounding Jerusalem, then those days are not also somewhere in our distant future. Although so many Christians desperately want both to be true, they can't be if we are holding Jesus and the apostles to their word, in the literary, audience relevant context in which they were continually speaking.

It would appear that the teachings of spiritual principles by Jesus have been incorrectly merged together with the New Testament subject of a first-century specific regional war between Jerusalem and Rome. Merging these two very separate subjects together in such a seamless fashion, I sincerely believe, is one of the main culprits of the construction of some of the most exegetically schizophrenic doctrines of current mainstream Christianity.

The Shocking, Unavoidable Conclusion

Preachers are telling people there is an imminent, grand, utopian, science fiction-like event that is just around the corner from happening that is absolutely never going to happen. The afternoon sky is not going to open up like a scroll with beams of sunlight and glory, and the Jesus of the Bible is not going to come down through actual clouds riding on a white stallion with a sword in his mouth. Graves are not going to open up down at the local cemetery, and missing airline pilots are not going to be raptured from their cockpits. In short, Jesus is not (physically) coming back here, not soon, not ever. I can now honestly say from my heart that this is not a blasphemous statement, but simple, biblical truth. According to the Bible, what I had been taught about all of this was completely wrong, and I now knew it. Some, even after this very compelling study, will hold on tight to their inherited doctrines. I cannot.

List of Recommended Books and Resources:

Last Days Madness by Gary DeMar

The Book of Revelation Made Easy by Kenneth L. Gentry

Matthew 24 Fulfilled by John L. Bray

The Days of Vengeance by David Chilton

The Olivet Discourse Made Easy by Kenneth L. Gentry

Christianity's Greatest Dilemma by Glenn L. Hill

The Last Days According to Jesus by R.C. Sproul

Before Jerusalem Fell by Kenneth L. Gentry

The Elements Shall Melt with Fervent Heat by Don K. Preston

AD 70 – A Shadow of the 'Real' End? by Don K. Preston

Last Days Identified by Don K. Preston

Destruction of Jerusalem by George Peter Holford

Early Church and End of the World by Gary DeMar and Francis Gumerlock

First Century Events in Chronological Order by Ed Stevens

Have Heaven and Earth Passed Away? by Don K. Preston

He Came as a Thief in the Night by Don K. Preston

The Parousia by James Stewart Russell

The information is not hard to find. We just have to want to find it.

Three

THE DOCTRINE OF HELL AND ETERNAL SEPARATION

Did Jesus teach of people going to a (physical) burning "hell?"

Another vanishing subject is hell, which has all but faded from being addressed at the pulpit. This is because many church leaders, with a healthy degree of exegetical integrity, have discovered that much of their predecessor's interpretations were sorely flawed. It is a well-established fact among scholars that the word "hell" was not in any of the original manuscripts, but was added to the Bible in early England. The English word "hell" comes from a pagan source, not the ancient writings of the Bible. The word "hell" is not found anywhere in the Torah, (which is the Christian's Old Testament). The word has completely disappeared from the Old Testament Scriptures in most leading Bibles. Why? Because the best scholarship demands it. The word "hell" actually comes from the Teutonic "hele," the mythological goddess of the underworld hell of northern Europe, not from the roots of Christianity. Did you know that? I certainly didn't know that. Wouldn't that be important?

The Word "Sheol"

Whenever the word "Sheol" is used in the Bible it simply means "place of the dead" or "the grave." It is the same word used throughout the entire Old Testament. Are we to conclude that all the Old Testament patriarchs are in hell?

What about Hades?

The word "Hades" occurs but eleven times in the New Testament, and has been translated as "hell" ten times, and as "grave" once. The word simply means "concealed or invisible." It has exactly the same meaning as Sheol, literally "the grave, or death;" and figuratively "destruction, downfall, calamity, or punishment in this world," with no intimation whatsoever of torment beyond the grave. Such is the meaning in every passage of the Old Testament containing the word "sheol" or "Hades," whether translated "hell," "grave," or "pit." This is also the invariable meaning of "Hades" in the New Testament. To translate "Hades" by the word "hell" as it is done ten times out of eleven in the New Testament, is very improper.

What about Gehenna?

It is common knowledge among all seasoned Christian theologians that Gehenna was actually referring to a huge garbage dump outside of first-century Jerusalem in the valley of Hinnom. It burned 24 hours a day and was where all things useless and valueless were thrown. It was also a place where outcasts and lepers gathered, trying to find food in the dump amongst the rotting garbage where there were worms and maggots. Long before the first destruction of Jerusalem, it was a graveyard, and then it was further profaned after it was used as a place for sacrificing children to pagan gods. Then, in the first century, it became Jerusalem's garbage dump. When Jesus used this word, he used it symbolically. Being put in the garbage dump would certainly show a completely different meaning than hell fire. First-century Jews knew exactly what Jesus was talking about when He referred to the city's garbage dump. It was also a place where the unclaimed bodies of paupers and vagrants were thrown to be burned.

Losing Hell

Once you take away hell and eternal separation from God, you automatically force people to have to rethink their entire religion. The scripture-based revelation that there is no hell or eternal banishment from God doesn't change just a few things; it literally destroys a great deal of what we were once so sure the gospel was all about. It is therefore understandable how, out of a lengthy list of old doctrines that evangelical Christians are willing to give up, the fear-driven belief of an eternal death sentence punishment is not one of them. Why? Because much of Christianity is wrongfully based on a 'reward and punishment' system. Many people are (actually) afraid of losing their fear. Please think about what I just said. They literally believe that if they lost their fear of God, they would also lose their reverence for God. Nothing of course could be further from the truth.

In this chapter I will clearly show that what the church has been teaching about hell is in sharp, disagreeable contrast to the Bible's original language and intent. Even the most casual study reveals this, and yet this fear-based doctrine is so deeply ingrained that many will not relinquish it as the sick, twisted, dark fable that it is, even if overwhelming biblical support is given. For centuries, no one questioned the church's (literalist) westernized interpretations of these ancient Middle Eastern (mostly metaphorical-seasoned) conversations. The only difference now, especially in this information age, is that the vast number of Christians who are seriously researching this subject has reached critical mass, to the extent that yesterday's theologians and scholars are no longer being allowed to just ignore what the parishioners are now uncovering.

Questions About "Hell"

With permission from Gary Amirault, the following numbered paragraphs are gleanings from one of the most comprehensive Christian perspective resources on this subject: tentmaker.org. I have numbered these so they can easily be referenced when discussing them with others.

    1. If hell, as a place of everlasting torture, was the real fate of all mankind unless they did something here on earth to prevent it, why didn't God make that warning plain right at the beginning of the Bible? God said the penalty for eating of the Tree of the Knowledge of Good and Evil was death. He did not define death as eternal life being forever tortured in fire. If hell was real, why didn't Moses warn about this fate in over 600 laws, ordinances, and warnings? The Mosaic Law simply stated blessings and cursings in this lifetime for failure to keep the Law. If hell was real, and if Paul was commissioned by God to preach the gospel to the nations, why did Paul never mention hell even once except to declare victory over it? (1 Cor. 15:55, the word "death" in this passage is the word "Hades").

    2. If hell is real and it is a place of being eternally separated from God, why does David say in the King James Bible, "Though I make my bed in Hell (Sheol) lo, Thou art there?" Most Christian Bibles no longer have the word hell in the Old Testament. The KJV, written over 350 years ago, is an exception. The Jews do not put the word "hell" in their English translations of the Hebrew Scriptures, and the leading English Christian Bibles have removed it because it is not in the originals. Most Christian scholars now acknowledge it should never have been put there in the first place.

    3. If hell doesn't exist in the Old Testament, how could Jesus and his disciples teach first-century Jews that salvation was deliverance from a place that is not even found in their scriptures? Or could it be that Jesus never taught such a concept in the first place? Since some English translations use the word "hell" for the Greek word "Gehenna," in the New Testament, why didn't this same place (Gehenna) get translated into "hell" in the many places where it appears in the Hebrew form *"ga ben Hinnom"* in the Old Testament? If the Jews did not understand this valley as a symbol of everlasting torture, why do some English

translations give this word such a meaning? And who burned whom in this valley? And what was God's response for Israel doing such a horrible thing to their children? (Jer. 32:33-35). And how could God say, "Such a thing never entered His mind" if in fact He is going to do the very same thing to most of His own children?

4. If hell is real, and all died, not because of their transgressions, but because of Adam's transgression (Rom 5:18), why do many Christians not see what is written, that "even so through one Man's righteous act the free gift came to all men, resulting in justification of life" (Rom. 5:18)? This scripture declares that all are justified due to Christ's righteous act. No one decided to die in Adam, it was reckoned to us. Equally, no one decided to receive eternal life; it is also reckoned to us. A thorough understanding of Romans chapter five carefully comparing several English translations would be a very good exercise. The omission of the definite article "the" in Rom. 5:15 before the word "many" in some translations has caused some great misunderstanding of this most important chapter of the Bible. If hell is real and is the fate of all mankind because of Adam's transgression, if all are not saved through the last Adam, Jesus Christ, does that not make the transgression of the first Adam greater than the redeeming act of Jesus (Rom. Chapter 5)? If hell is real, in Romans 5:19, the "many" who were made sinners were actually "all" of the human race. Why is the "many" who were made righteous not equally "all" of the human race? "For as by one man's disobedience many were made sinners, so also by one Man's obedience many will be made righteous."

5. If Christians really believed in hell, would they not spend their entire lives trying to snatch their friends and relatives from the burning flames? Why don't they do this? On a daily basis, people who claim to believe in hell walk away from the lady at the coffee shop, the guy at the garage, the clerk at the mall, the woman in the bank window, and the flight attendant without saying one word about Jesus or hell. How can they do this? The answer is simple: they somehow know in their hearts that it is not necessary.

6. If hell is real, and easy to define and find in the Bible, why did the translators of the original 1611 King James Bible find it so difficult to define Hades? They put hell in the text at Revelation 20:13 and "Or, grave" in the margins,

while putting "grave" in the text and "Or, hell" in the margins in 1 Cor. 15:55? Seems they couldn't make up their minds whether Hades meant "hell" or "grave." Recent editions have removed the marginal readings, thus avoiding the embarrassment.

7. If hell is real and everlasting, why is it thrown into the Lake of Fire to be destroyed? Why is hell never called the Lake of Fire, nor the Lake of Fire ever called hell, if they are the same thing? If hell is referring to a place of eternal torment, then why is the word "aionion" (in verses like Matthew 18:8), which is used in the original language, translated as "eternal" in our modern Bibles when it does not mean "eternal?" The word comes from the Greek root "aion" meaning "age." This fact combined with the various uses of Greek words derived from the root "aion," show that "aionion" does not mean "eternal," but rather a finite period of time.

8. If hell is a real place of everlasting punishment and if Jesus died in our place to save us from this fate, wouldn't Jesus have to be eternally punished if in fact He took our full punishment upon Himself? But He's not being eternally punished. He died, which is what the penalty of the wages of sin is – death -- not everlasting life of unending torture, or eternal death, or annihilation.

9. If hell is real, and the greatest part of mankind eventually goes there, wouldn't Jesus be considered a great failure considering the fact He was sent to save the whole world? Since probably less than one percent of the world's population ever got born again and stayed on the straight and narrow, doesn't this fly in the face of Jesus' words which says He leaves the ninety-nine to find the one and doesn't give up until He finds it (Luke 15:4)?

10. If hell is real, does that mean that motherly love is more powerful and enduring than God's love? Do you know of normal mothers (or fathers) who would endlessly torment most of their kids?

In Julie Ferwerda's book *Raising Hell,* she tells us how she was raised in the church to believe our heavenly Father expects better and more loving and tolerant behaviors from us than He does from Himself, such as: "Never pay back evil for evil to anyone" (Rom. 12:17); "Love your enemies and pray for those who persecute you" (Matt. 5:44); "Love your enemies, do good to those who hate you" (Luke 6:27); "Be merciful, just as your Father is merciful"

(Luke 6:36); "Bless those who curse you, pray for those who mistreat you" (Luke 6:28); "Do not be overcome by evil, but overcome evil with good" (Rom. 12:21); "Love your enemies, and do good, and lend, expect nothing in return; and your reward will be great, and you will be sons of the Most High" (Luke 6:35).

Julie makes a poignant observation by saying, "God asks me to forgive my enemies, to be kind to them, to show them mercy, and to overcome their evil with good, yet He is ultimately not going to forgive His enemies, to be kind to them, to show them mercy, and to overcome their evil with good? If this is what our Father is really like, and we are to imitate Him as sons of the Most High, shouldn't we then turn our backs on our enemies, damn them, and build torture chambers for them?"

But wait a minute. Doesn't it say in Romans 5:8 that God showed His love for us while we were still sinners and that we were reconciled to God while we were still His enemies? If He did this for you and me, why should He not do it for everyone? Doesn't this passage in effect say that God has already overcome His children's evil with good, even if we haven't observed it or even fully understood it yet? If man does wrong in returning evil for evil, would not God do wrong if He was to do the same (Romans 12:20, 21)? Would not endless punishment be the return of evil for evil? As we are commanded to overcome evil with good, may we not safely infer that God will do the same? Would the infliction of endless punishment be overcoming evil with good? If God loves His enemies now, will he not always love them? Is God a changeable being (Jam. 1:17)?

11. If hell is real, how does the threat of endlessly torturing us convince us that God loves us and that we should love Him with all our heart, soul, mind and strength? If God only loves those who love Him, what better is He than the sinner (Luke 6:32-33)? Can you really call eternally torturing your own children love? Since love worketh no ill (Rom. 13:10), can God inflict, or cause, or allow to be inflicted, an endless ill? If the demands of divine justice are opposed to the requirements of mercy, is not God divided against Himself? If the requirements of mercy are opposed to the demands of the justice of God, can His kingdom stand (Mark 3:24)? If hell is real, does not judgment triumph over mercy and thus contradict this scripture (Jam. 2:13)?

12. If hell is real, and God is our Father and our potter (Is. 64:8, 9), did He make mostly junk? Are most of the children He raised misfits worthy only to be thrown away and endlessly tortured? Do we not hold parents responsible for their children's outcome? If we use the same standards toward God's fathering abilities, according to the doctrine of endless punishment, our Father did a very poor job in raising His children. We wouldn't think of sending our pets to such a place, yet don't blink an eye at the thought of God sending His very own children to such a place. If hell is real and sin is infinite, can it be true that "where sin abounded grace did much more abound" (Rom. 5:20)?

Early Church History on Hell

If hell was a teaching of the early church, why did the fourth-century church appoint an avowed Universalist as the President of the second council of the church in Constantinople (Gregory Nazianzen, 325-381)? Church leaders, as late as the fourth century AD, acknowledged that the majority of Christians believed in the salvation of all mankind. The first comparatively complete systematic statement of Christian doctrine ever given to the world by Clement of Alexandria, AD 180, contains the tenet of universal salvation. The first complete presentation of Christianity (Origen, AD 220) contains the doctrine of universal salvation.

Why didn't the church teach the hell doctrine until after the church departed from reading the Bible in Greek and Hebrew, substituting Latin in its stead several centuries after Christ's death?

Not one single Christian writer of the first three centuries declared universalism as a heresy. Not a single one of the early creeds expressed any idea contrary to universal restoration, or in favor of everlasting punishment in hell. No Church council for the first five hundred years condemns universalism as heresy, although they did make many declarations of heresy on other teachings. Most of the early church's leading scholars and most revered saints advocate universal salvation. The most prominent Universalists of the early church were born into Christian families and were most highly revered by their peers, while those who advocated hell came from paganism and confessed they were among the vilest (Tertullian and Augustine).

If hell was found in the original Greek manuscripts of the Bible, why is it that it was primarily those church leaders who either couldn't read Greek (Minucius Felix, Tertullian), or hated Greek as in the case of Augustine, that the doctrine of hell was advocated? Those early church leaders familiar with the Greek and Hebrew (the original languages of the Bible) saw universal salvation in those texts. Those who advocated hell got it from the Latin, not from the original Greek and Hebrew. Who would more likely be correct: those who could read the original languages of the Bible, or those who read a Latin translation made by one man (Jerome)?

Most leading historians acknowledge that the early church was dominated by universalism. Four out of six theological schools from AD 170 to 430 taught universal salvation while the only one that taught hell was in Carthage, Africa, again where Latin was the teaching language, not Greek. Why didn't Epiphanius (c. 315-403), known as the "hammer of heretics" who listed 80 heresies of his time, not list universalism among those heresies? Most historians would acknowledge today that Origen was perhaps the most outstanding example of early universalism in the church. When Methodius, Eusibius, Pamphilus, Marcellus, Eustathius, and Jerome made their lists of Origen's heresies, why wasn't universalism among them? Could it be perhaps that it wasn't a heresy in the original church?

It was not until the sixth century when Justinian, a half-pagan emperor, tried to make universalism a heresy. Interestingly, most historians will acknowledge that Justinian's reign was among the most cruel and ruthless. It is well known by historians of the early church writings that Universal Reconciliation was the main, majority belief, and was taught authoritatively by all the major theologians of those first few centuries in the churches that the Apostle Paul founded.

The False Concept of Hell Violates Everything That Is Reasonable

The false concept of hell violates the nature of God, which is unconditional Love. It violates the wisdom of God, the pleasure of God, the promises of God, the oath of God, the power of God. It negates the full power of the cross of Christ. It goes against the testimony of the prophets; it violates the testimony of Jesus Christ and his apostles. It violates the scriptures in their original languages. It violates the writings of the early church leaders who read the scriptures in the original languages. It goes against our conscience, and it goes against our hearts.

Great theologians and scholars have come to the same conclusion. Among them are people like William Barclay, William Law, Karl Barth, Schleiermacher, Bishop Westcott, Lightfoot, Canon F.W. Farrar, John A.T. Robinson, Andrew Murray, and Andrew Jukes, and many more.

Please refer to tentmaker.org for deeper Christian perspective studies on this subject.

What About the Lazarus Story (Luke 16:19-31)?

Many preachers have wrongfully used this parable as support for the hell doctrine by claiming that it is a literal story. In doing so, they unknowingly open up some very awkward scenarios. If we are to take this parable as a literal story, then we must come to the conclusion that wealthy people go to hell and poor beggars end up in a place called "Abraham's bosom." The rich man is not depicted as a sinner, nor is Lazarus described as a righteous man. Also, if this is a literal story about heaven and hell, then those who are in hell will be able to converse with those in heaven. Those in heaven will supposedly be able to see and hear their friends and loved ones being tortured in hell. When was the last time you heard that version from the pulpit? When we incorrectly turn a parable into a literal story, we create a contradictive dilemma.

If we take the time and the care to revisit this passage in the context it was written in, considering the entire teaching, and to what audience it was being addressed to, we will quickly discover a much different story. It is actually the last part of a five-part teaching Jesus was giving to the Pharisees and the gentiles at the same time. It starts with the parable of the lost sheep, and then moves on to the lost coin, the lost son, the shrewd manager, and lastly, the Lazarus parable. The Pharisees were very upset about Jesus including the gentiles in the blessing, showing them mercy, acceptance, and even healing them. To them the gentiles were like dogs that should only be consoled by their own kind. They thought that Jesus shouldn't even have been talking to them.

All of these parables are about the same subject. The older son in the prodigal son parable represents the Pharisees, and the lost son is the gentiles. In the shrewd manager parable, the Pharisees knew that Jesus was rebuking them for being poor stewards of God's blessings.

What the Pharisees Understood

1. The rich man was dressed in purple (symbol of kingship and belonging to the kingdom of David), and also in fine linen (symbol of priesthood, being referred to as a descendant of Abraham).

2. Why five brothers? The tribe of Judah received the kingdom and the priesthood. Judah had five brothers. What so many modern-day preachers are still confused about, the first-century Pharisees were not. They knew that Jesus was talking about them when he spoke of the rich man dressed in purple and fine linen with five brothers.

3. Lazarus. This is the only parable where Jesus actually names one of the characters. The Hebrew translation for "Lazarus" is "Eleazar" which means "God helped us." The parable shows that Lazarus has some sort of relationship with Abraham, for he ends up in his bosom. The text also shows him as a gentile. He was also a steward because he is now eligible for being in Abraham's bosom. In Genesis chapter 15, Abram's head servant Eleazar fits all of these characteristics. The Pharisees knew that Lazarus represented the gentile nations who were outside of the inheritance of Abraham.

The parable of Lazarus is not (in any stretch of the imagination) about hell or heaven, but a very uncomfortable teaching primarily to the Pharisees about gentiles now being included in the family, and also heirs of Abraham. The gentiles were probably elated about this news, but the Pharisees were obviously outraged. In short, the Lazarus parable was someone else's ancient story, not ours.

What About Dark and Scary NDE Testimonies?

I believe in the afterlife, and I know that near death experiences are real, because I had one myself. I sincerely believe that the only part of NDEs anyone can believe for doctrine's sake is the first two or three seconds where they all describe the initial leaving of the body and their eternal consciousness rising, perhaps a tunnel of sorts with light, the feeling of weightlessness, peace, and an unexplainable oneness with everything in existence. Everything else in every single story differs. The reason for this in my honest opinion is because much of what often comes next for each person is being manufactured by the individual's brain (because of every thought during one's lifetime of overheard conversations, teachings, imaginings of death, the afterlife, heaven, hell, rejoining loved ones, hopes, fears, desires, doctrines, beliefs, etc.). A good example is the little boy of whose (church going) parents wrote a popular scripture peppered book where the boy ends up seeing a future battle of Armageddon that he must now warn us all about. Coincidently, he had sat in church services and heard all about such things his entire childhood life.

Some people see light beings, some see words in the sky, some walk on flowers that pop up after you've stepped on them, some see Jesus, some see Lao Tzu, and some see sparkly, neon ocean waves washing in over their feet. Some, in that state of higher consciousness, are even able to access information about the family of which they couldn't possibly have known before. Some fly over valleys and lush, green meadows like an eagle; some see scary monsters and screaming; some see Grandpa and the family dog; some see streets of gold and an actual throne (that surprisingly looks a lot like an early English Medieval times throne); some see a river and a field of onion plants; and, believe it or not, some even see that really attractive blonde girl they always wished they'd asked out back in high school, sitting on a brand new Honda Goldwing motorcycle, with the old Abba song "Knowing Me, Knowing You" playing in the background.

Final point being made; None of the testimonies beyond that initial two or three seconds can be used in any way to build doctrine or even to establish something specific about a certain religion. They tell us more about the person than what awaits the rest of us beyond death's door.

"Yeah, But What About…?"

At this point, some may be entertaining the typical barrage of questions this all creates. Everything from "Are there then no consequences for our actions?" to questions like "What about people in history like Hitler?" Another popular response is "Ken, are you saying that people can basically go around doing whatever they want and are still going to heaven?" I will address each of these questions and more in the following chapters, but for now, let me introduce the idea and possibility that many of the fundamental doctrines we have been taught about both the 'here and now' and the hereafter are significantly flawed. I am also asking you, just for the time being, to imagine all the teachings of Jesus being about the 'here and now,' not the afterlife.

If there were a place called "hell," then our relationship with our Creator is not based on unconditional love, but on 'reward and punishment,' which would then indeed be based on the "fear of loss and the possibility of gain."

Suggested books:

Raising Hell by Julie Ferwerda

What the Hell by Jackson Baer

Spiritual Terrorism by Boyd C. Purcell, Ph. D.

Hope Beyond Hell by Gerry Beauchemin

I Didn't Want It to Come to This

Here I stand now realizing that I have to completely rethink all these things that my predecessors had completely missed. And yes, there were many doctrinal issues that I often wished could just stay unchanged in my mind. I didn't want to have to rethink my entire religion, but if I was to be honest with myself that was indeed what I was now facing. The only other choice was to sweep all these uncomfortable passages under the church carpet like I had done for years, and basically go on lying to myself. But when you are no longer afraid of truth regardless of where it might lead, you will most certainly end up in places you once swore you would never go.

I was beginning to realize for the first time in my life that many of the doctrines I had been taught were truly not based on exegetical weight, audience relevance, or literary context, but upon long held, fiercely protected, 'hand me down' doctrines of men.

Four
RE-THINKING MY INHERITED BELIEFS

Oh, the castles we have built near the incoming tide! When someone completely removes both a future return of Jesus and the fear-based doctrine of eternal punishment, we are left standing here in the realization that this is just the beginning of a very long and theologically awkward journey. Since it is a journey many of us really don't want to be necessary, or true, our first instinct is often denial, and our second instinct is a sort of militantly implemented ignoring of the facts. Here is a short list of some word for word reactions I have personally encountered.

"I don't believe any of this, and I am not buying those books or looking up those verses."

"I have a very simple faith, and I know what I believe, and that's that."

"Well now, you can twist the scriptures into saying anything you want them to say."

"But what about this verse and what about that verse?"

"But if the church can be so wrong, then so can you, right?"

"Well, there are just a lot of things that we can't really know for sure until we get to heaven."

"Well, nobody really knows."

"I think we just need to stay focused on the main, most important things."

And last, but not least, "It doesn't matter."

All these responses have one thing in common: they all ignore the importance of uncomfortable truths rather than facing them head on with courage, intellectual honesty, and responsibility. Most of these responses are also motivated by a serious reluctance for change. For so many years, this was my story too. The main question is this: If we have been so wrong, for so long, about things that are so important, wouldn't we want to know about them so we can correct them at least for our grandchildren's sake? Or do we just keep on believing what we were taught simply because it is easier that way?

Unimportant Truths

Is there even such a thing? Actually, no, there is not. But when we are catapulted to a state of uncomfortable shock about a belief system that is suddenly revealed to be incorrect, we tend to impulsively change the subject to hopefully dampen the uneasiness, or at the very least start trying to downplay the discovery as 'not all that important' of an issue. Why is it that we actually expect more credibility from our children than we do of the clergy? We make doctrinal allowances for our church denomination in ways and degrees that we would never accept from our own kids. Speaking of making allowances, how many allowances are acceptable? Why would I continue attending or supporting a church that teaches so many things I disagree with? Believe it or not, many Christians do, hence the increasingly popular saying, "Oh I don't agree with everything my pastor teaches, but I do agree on the important, fundamental stuff."

The church however doesn't make such gracious allowances for differing theological views, nor will they tolerate them. For example, if someone is discussing the coming of the Son of Man in an interpretive fashion that differs from the official position of the church, it is often conveniently defined as "wrangling on about doctrinal issues that can only lead to dissension among the saints, or distraction from the 'real' work of the Lord." But, if the pastor invites a denomination approved special speaker to do a five-night series on the same exact subject, that is sold as "Fresh, new insights on the book of Revelation and the End Times."

Pulling Out the Apostle Paul Card

Unfortunately, it is still typical to hear pastors warning their flocks to not even listen to someone who is sharing an interpretation that differs from their denomination's official position. Regardless of the subject at hand, here are some of the verses often used to shut down any theological positions that differ from the church's views.

> "Avoid idle chatter" (2 Tim. 2:16).
>
> "The time will come when they will not endure sound doctrine; but wanting to have their ears tickled, they will accumulate to themselves teachers in accordance to their own desires; and will turn away their ears from the truth, and will turn aside to myths." (2 Tim. 4:3-4, also 2 Thess. 2:9, 10).
>
> "Keep your eye on those who cause dissensions and hindrances contrary to the teaching which you learned, and turn away from them. For such men are slaves, not of our Lord Christ but of their own appetites; and by their smooth and flattering speech they deceive the hearts of the unsuspecting" (Rom. 16:17-18).
>
> "But even though we, or an angel from heaven, should preach to you a gospel contrary to that which we have preached to you, let him be accursed" (Galatians 1:8).
>
> "Shun foolish controversies and genealogies and strife and disputes about the law; for they are unprofitable and worthless" (Titus 3:9).

There are, of course, many more, including "doctrines of demons" (1 Timothy 4:1), but the point I'm trying to make is that preachers continually pull out these ancient sentences to hopefully counteract any modern-day doctrine based, controversial discussions that are brewing within the church walls. This never did ring of freedom and openness to me, but rather a fear based protectionism that is more about control, all conveniently cast as a concerned shepherd cautiously looking out for the flock.

Statements of Faith and Honesty

On any church website you will find a section of "Core Beliefs." These "What We Believe" statements cover subjects like the virgin birth, the resurrection, the trinity, divine healing, a future return of Jesus, and several other things. Since they are stated in such a matter-of-fact fashion, most people have never truly questioned them. Like the 1972 song by Stevie Wonder, "Superstition," we have been coached to "believe in things we don't understand." Some things in life, when they are thoroughly explained, produce a response like "Oh, okay, I can see now how that makes sense." But many of our inherited religious beliefs not only do not make sense, but if we are to be honest, are also completely illogical and often contrary to nature itself. There were so many things about my evangelical Christian faith that never did seem rational, but I was told, "That is why it is called faith."

But what if we stepped back and reviewed some of our inherited beliefs from a skeptic's logic-based point of view? How would our doctrines look through their eyes? And could we learn anything valuable from such a revelation? Well, let's find out.

Well-Assembled Stack of Rocks

Two questions:

1. Does Christianity teach that God once required animal sacrifices in the Old Testament?

2. Do Christians consider the laws of Moses to have been inventions of Moses, or instructions to Moses directly from God?

I would have to confess that the origins of my belief system could truthfully be described like this. At some point after God created 500 billion galaxies, He picked one of those galaxies as His favorite galaxy, and amongst that one galaxy's one hundred billion solar systems, also picked one favorite solar system, planet, continent, regional area, and then created a favorite people. When the people disobeyed the rules, God basically said, "I'm going to need someone to go get an animal, kill it, and burn it on a stack of rocks in order for Me to be happy." In short, "You owe Me for breaking My rules by sinning, so something must die." Although you will be hard pressed to ever find an evangelical Christian who will explain it all like that, it is essentially what most Christians do actually believe. In ancient days, this began what eventually became not only ancient Judaism, but also penal substitutionary Christianity. Even to this very day, many people actually think it is their job to somehow make God happy, and some of them still add the words "or else."

Is it even possible that it could have been man who thought that perhaps killing and offering a dead animal as a sacrifice might appease their concept of a God? Was there really some sort of humanoid, Zeus-like figure getting together somewhere in outer space with Jesus and the Holy Spirit declaring, "Let us make man in our own image?" And did such a … Being literally 'breathe into man's nostrils'? Or did ancient men on our planet conceptualize a God according to their image and likeness?

I had been shaped and formed into a lifestyle ideology where one believes there is an invisible, magic kingdom of spiritual enlightenment that only Christians can see, enter, and experience. We had an ancient Middle Eastern spiritual leader who would one-day re-enter earth's atmosphere on an actual horse, sporting a gigantic, cubed golden city two-thirds the size of our moon. And we believed in a Creator who either terminates or eternally tortures any and all humans throughout history who did not love Him correctly according to some ancient, Middle Eastern written procedure and protocol. Many people from my background are insulted when someone from their own camp explains it all in that brutally-honest fashion, but it is what most evangelicals believe.

Doctrine of the Trinity

There are many different views on this subject. At one time I actually believed there was only one view, the 'correct' view, and that the 'fact' of the trinity was not to be questioned, especially if you wanted to be seen as someone who had any biblical knowledge or intelligence. Many of the opponents of the trinity doctrine strongly feel that deifying Jesus actually keeps us from seeing and understanding some of the very fundamental essences of what Jesus was trying to teach us about a 'oneness' with the Father… a oneness that Jesus himself actually prayed that we would all hopefully experience. The pro-trinity people claim that is not only preposterous, but shows a great lack of understanding of the scriptures. But when you take the time and the effort to fully investigate the anti-trinity view, you actually discover a greater bulk of (Bible-based, in-context) common sense and sound reasoning than the pro-trinity view. This, at first, I will have to admit, was quite shocking to me.

We have all heard the egg example: shell, white, yolk yet one egg; or the three-leaf clover yet one clover. Or H2O: ice, water and steam. And we have also heard that we are triune beings, body, soul, and spirit, like God is Father, Son, and Spirit.

The Trinity Did Not Originate with Ancient Judaism or Christianity

Without too much research one will quickly find that the concept of a "triune God" originated in ancient Egypt, and they probably inherited it from a civilization even more ancient. In Indian religion there is the Trinitarian group of Brahma, Vishna, and Shiva; in Egyptian religion there is the group of Kneph, Phthas, and Osiris. In Phoenicia the trinity of gods were Ulomus, Ulosuros, and Eliun. In Greece they were Zeus, Poseidon, and Aidoneus. In Rome they were Jupiter, Neptune, and Pluto. In Babylonia and Assyria they were Anos, Illinos, and Aos. Among Celtic nations they were called Kriosan, Biosena, and Siva, and in Germanic nations they were called Thor, Wodan, and Fricco.

To my surprise, a little research revealed that this doctrine was imposed on the church in the fourth century during the Council of Nicaea, but it certainly was romanced into many hymns, romantic sermons, and lofty commentaries in the early 1900's. There are many verses in which trinity proponents argue that Jesus is claiming to be a part of a 'Godhead,' but upon closer examination, when taken in context, it appears rather to be a matter of Jesus claiming to represent the true character of God.

Even in my late fifties, I am still amazed at how a semi-objective, in-depth study of any particular doctrine can quickly produce a completely different conclusion than what a thousand preachers have taught for years. We have been conditioned to believe that if the majority believes in something, then it can be trusted as true and never in need of questioning. The trinity debate is a very lengthy and in-depth process for sure. After an enormous amount of research and study on both sides of this argument, I had to admit to myself that the doctrine of the trinity is a product of man's multi-dimensional, puzzle-like, literary construction of a God who sends Himself to appease Himself, prays to Himself, but then obeys Himself by offering Himself as a sacrifice to Himself, supposedly saving mankind from Himself, and then returning to Himself. I remember hearing fellow Christians parrot the saying "The One from whom we needed to be saved is the One who saved us." But that didn't really make a whole lot of sense to me. The ironic thing is that the people making such a statement actually believed they were saying something spiritually romantic.

Jesus clearly stated that he saw himself as less than the Father, and in many places subservient to the Father. Jesus said "My Father is greater than I", and repeatedly makes statements of NOT being God (John 14:28, Mark 10:18, and many others), so how is it possible for Jesus to be part of a trinity of which he is an equal to when he states God is greater than himself? In John 10:30 Jesus says, "I and the Father are one". The verse does not say, "I and the Father am one God". There are scripture verses that do tell us that there is indeed only one God. But there are no verses even suggesting that God has three parts, nor three functions, nor three persons.

I see Jesus speaking of being one with the Father as being a oneness that all of humanity would hopefully one day enjoy with one another and with God. If I tell you that my wife and I are "one", I certainly do not mean that I am my wife as well as myself. One of the primary missions of Jesus was to open man's eyes to a new and better way of seeing themselves, each other, and their relationship with God. He taught that we could be one with the Father 'just as he was'. How is it that we have missed that? If we can be "one" with the Father "just as" Jesus was "one" with the Father, then would that make us a "part of the trinity"? Does that not sound silly?

After actually taking the time and the effort of studying the proponent's views of the trinity, I walked away even more confused than when I began. To be completely honest, I would have to say that the trinity proponents are promoting, maintaining, and protecting a 'hand me down' doctrine that is not based on a larger bulk of exegetical integrity than the anti-trinity position, but mostly upon the inherited romance of the wildly misinterpreted invention itself. Anyone who truly tries to study both positions objectively will clearly discover the anti-trinity view containing the vast bulk of scriptural support in literary context. There is a reason large books are written on this subject by Christian apologists. In my honest opinion, it is required in order to keep such a bizarre construction afloat. I have a funny feeling that we hold on tight to some particular doctrines for the main reason that by losing that doctrine all sorts of uncomfortable things happen to other doctrines that need it for support. Therefore 'not so accurate' doctrines oft times get preserved and fiercely protected for the wrong reasons. I sincerely believe this to be the case here. I would strongly encourage my readers to take the time and effort to study both sides of this subject on their own, and then ask themselves which side is based mostly on literary-context scripture and which is based mostly on romance of an interpretive cherry-picked concept.

We Believe What We Were Told To Believe (by really smart people)

Nowhere in the Bible is the word "trinity" or Godhead" found, nor the word "three" as describing God. Never is God said to be a "person", nor is the Holy Spirit ever called God.

Here is a list of Bible verses which bring into serious question of Jesus being "God"...

> Matthew 3:16-17; 8:29; 11:27; 12:18; 14:33; 16:16-17; 17:5; 27:54, Mark 5:7; 15:39, Luke 1:32; 1:35; 8:28; 9:35; 10:22, John 1:13; 1:18; 1:34; 1:49; 3:16; 5:19-23; 5:37; 6:40; 6:69; 8:18; 8:42; 10:15; 10:36; 11:4; 12:49-50;

14:13; 14:23; 14:28; 16:17; 17:1-16; 20:17; 20:31, Acts 2:22-24; 3:13; 3:26; 9:20, Romans 1:4; 5:10; 8:29, 1 Corinthians 11:3; 15:28, 2 Corinthians 1:19, Galatians 4:4, Philippians 2:9, Colossians 1:13, 1 Thessalonians 1:10, 1 Timothy 2:5, Hebrews 1:2; 2:9; 4:14; 5:7-8, 1 Peter 1:3, 2 Peter 1:17, 1 John 1:3; 2:22; 3:23; 4:10; 4:14-15; 5:11-12, 2 John 1:9, Revelation 2:18

Penal Substitutionary Theory

My friend Joshua Tongol (founder of joshuatongol.com) helped me understand this doctrine. Here is the basic premise of this belief called Penal Substitution: The Creator of 500 billion galaxies (each containing 100 billion solar systems) sends His only son to die for our sins in this galaxy, in our solar system, to somehow satisfy the justice of God. This teaching insists that Jesus basically came to die in our place, taking upon himself our punishment, and our penalty, because he loves us. God is holy (in a legal sense), and since man sinned, he has broken the law and therefore is guilty. God supposedly cannot allow sin to go unpunished because of His holiness. And since He is just, justice requires punishment; hence His wrath must be satisfied. Most evangelical Christians can readily relate to having been taught this version of the crucifixion.

We were also taught that God is love, which is supposedly why He sends His only son to die (as a blood sacrifice) for our sins. The way this has been interpreted by some is that it was also at that very moment when God, because He is holy and supposedly cannot look upon sin, turned His face away from His son, abandoning him, so he could be fully punished with the full weight of the sin of all mankind. Although this all sounds like something out of the movie *Lord of the Rings*, we trustingly believed it all as if it were a fact. We can spin and romanticize this interpretation of the scriptures until the cows come home, but what it actually articulates is that we were spared from God's wrath. But haven't we clearly established that "wrath" throughout the New Testament was a first-century only eschatological issue? Have these two very separate events been incorrectly merged into the same story?

Just recently, I chanced upon a Christian radio station where a worship song was playing: "Thank you Jesus for your sacrifice; the Father's wrath satisfied." In this song, a congregation, with their hands lifted toward heaven, had no idea that the words they were devotionally chanting were so theologically incorrect, nor that 'wrath' is a topic exclusive to first-century events that have nothing to do with the crucifixion.

The first signs of this idea that Jesus came to die for our sins was Anselm's Satisfaction Theory of Atonement and then later developed into becoming more 'penal' when John Calvin came on the scene. An English monk formulated another philosophy called the Ransom Theory in AD 1098, a full 1000 years after Jesus died. Before then it was substitution atonement which took hold around 300 AD in which like the Job story, God tricked the devil to replace humans in hell with Jesus, but the devil didn't realize that Jesus was not under his power. Before that it was a varied mix of co-existing beliefs, most of which were Universalist in nature and that Jesus' death had to do with an expression of love in his life, rather than a substitution of any form of holy punishment. What amazes me most is how we have somehow been convinced that we are not qualified to do our own homework on these matters, and come up with our own conclusions. The rationale? We must trust the theologians, not ourselves.

Saved From God?

I was basically taught that Jesus came to save us from God. Even though many Christians will heatedly disagree with that assessment, when you got right down to the roots of the doctrine of penal substitution, it is precisely what is being taught. Growing up in the church I would never have described my faith in those terms, but when I really stopped to think about what I had been convinced to accept as reality, I would have to say that the above descriptions are strangely accurate. One of the most shocking-to-me things about sharing these observations is that many evangelicals reply, "No! That is not what I believe! I do not believe that Jesus came to save us from God!" But then they will get in their car and drive to a church where the pastor boldly teaches the very doctrines they just publicly denounced. Many people have not truly thought through the premises on which many of their fundamental doctrines are based on. For instance, some will claim that "God doesn't send people to hell," and that they "send themselves there." And yet it has not entered their minds that

God would have had to create this system that mankind is supposedly "sending themselves to". When the pastor says "God's wrath was satisfied", they have never really stopped to think for themselves what that also must say and mean about God.

Asking the Deeper Questions Means Going Deeper Than Is Comfortable

There's no way around it. If we really want the deeper answers, we will have to ask the deeper questions. But we can't stop there. If we go deep enough, we end up face-to-face with the *premises* those answers are based on. That's when you find that the foundational premises are where the investigation should really begin. But very few are courageous enough to go down there. We want all those fundamental foundations to be true and beyond questioning. And that's why we like to trustingly believe that all those scholars, theologians, preachers, and pastors couldn't possibly be wrong. That is the most popular route. Most theological debates do not get to the root of the trouble they are attempting to fix or clarify. Why? Because both parties are unwilling to question the premise the entire conversation is based upon.

Here is just one example of deeper questioning that challenges us to know why we believe what we do…

Church: "Jesus died for your sins."

Reasoning: "Why would that be necessary?"

Church: "Well, because man was born in sin."

Reasoning: "How did that happen, and what does that mean?"

Church: "Well, when Adam sinned it (magically) changed all of mankind somehow in a very dark way."

Reasoning: "How did it change mankind?"

Church: "Well, after that point they were all born sinners (in a 'fallen' state) and in need of a Savior."

Reasoning: "A Savior? Saved from what?"

Church: "Well, saved from their sins."

Reasoning: "Do you really mean saved from God?"

Church: "Well, yes, and no."

Reasoning: "But didn't you say that Jesus had to pay a price?"

Church: "Yes, Jesus paid for our sins with his life."

Reasoning: "So, whom was the payment being made to?"

Church: "Well, yes, it did also save us from God's wrath."

Reasoning: "Why would God need a torturous death of Jesus?"

Church: "Well, because God required it."

Reasoning: "Oh, like the ancient Aztecs?"

Church: "Look man, it should have been *us* on that cross, because that's what we deserve."

Reasoning: "Really? I deserve to be murdered for being born a human?!"

Church: "You don't understand. There had to be a blood sacrifice."

Reasoning: "Why would God require such a horrific thing?"

Church: "Well, it is more complicated than that. You see, in the Old Testament man was required to bring a lamb, and…"

Reasoning: "Why would God require such a strange thing?"

Church: "Well, because, um, the Bible says so."

Reasoning: "But that doesn't seem to make sense."

Church: "It doesn't have to make sense. That's why they call it faith."

Reasoning: "This all sounds like someone else's ancient, Middle Eastern religious stuff."

Church: "God's ways are not man's ways. You either believe the Bible or you don't."

Reasoning: "Dude. I'm not arguing. I'm just really and truly trying to understand it all."

There are a lot of church doctrines that many have long since accepted as fact (and as fully understood) that end in this 'not so understood' fashion when they are fully questioned. Most of them never come to this style of rigorous interrogation, but are just trustingly believed without a challenge. I do not mean to disrespect one's faith, but simply to ask the deeper questions that reveal the deeper answers. Personally, I am beginning to think that many of us have not thought many of the very fundamental doctrines of our faith completely through yet. I also think there are many who do not want to, and for obvious reasons.

In the Eyes of a Child

There is a reason why we somehow know that Mel Gibson's movie, *Passion of the Christ*, is probably not appropriate for grade-schoolers. There is something incorrect about mainstream Christianity's interpretation of the crucifixion, and I believe our hearts have always known it.

Even though doctrines like these are taught in the most sincere, reverential, poetic fashion, what children do in their own heads with it all, is another matter altogether. For me personally, it went something like this, "Honey, God doesn't want to kill you, mainly because He loves you so much. As a matter of fact, He loved you so much that He sent His only boy, which was actually Himself, to get tortured and killed instead. Why? Well, because He, um, required it, because, He is God, and, so that, well, um, Honey, it should have been *us* being crucified because that's what *we* deserve. But Jesus took our place on that cross, because that's just how ugly and bad and filthy and pathetic and deserving of death *we* really are. But, after Jesus prayed, to Himself, asking if there was any way out of this horrible treatment, He went ahead and paid that price, that death sentence for us and that is why we sing hymns like 'He paid a debt He did not owe, we owed a debt we could not pay' and so forth. And now, since He did die for us, we are really indebted to Him and devotionally owe Him every minute of our entire lives." Sound familiar?

Age of Accountability

When someone came to church with their precious one-year-old daughter with curly red hair, the man-made doctrine of the age of accountability had to be created to deal with what our hearts all knew about the little girl obviously being totally innocent. So what was the theological solution for this dilemma? The little girl must rely on her parents to hopefully explain to her, some time in her preteen years, just how dirty, helpless, deficient, fallen, incomplete, and undeserving of heaven she really is. That is if she is lucky enough to have parents that care enough to tell her about such an angry God from Whom we must all be saved.

Many people live this psychologically abusive version of God their entire lives. Some may say, "My church does not teach that!" But if they would check their denomination's doctrines and by-laws, they just may be surprised to find that their church teaches exactly that. Thankfully, in this very generation, there are scores of theologians and scholars rethinking new ways of looking at the crucifixion as they are closing in on more biblically accurate interpretations.

That Should Just About Do It

Throughout my years as a Christian, I have often pictured a bunch of eighteenth-century European scholars and Bible translators getting together in a room full of dusty, aging books, debating the true meanings of things like being 'born again,' 'salvation,' and 'eternal life.' Then, after much argument and more voting, I see them all coming to somewhat of an official church position:

1. One must confess their sins publicly in the church, preferably before the church leadership.

2. One must be genuinely repentant and sorry for the filthy, unworthy wretch that they are.

3. One must appeal to God above with the uttermost heartfelt sincerity for absolution (and legal acquittal) for being born a human, hence a sinner.

4. One must denounce Satan (an actual invisible being), and then place one's entire faith on Jesus and his sacrifice as the only way possible for one to escape hell and get off this planet alive when one's body expires.

"That should just about do it," says one of the old men with the eyepiece, which, over the centuries, has evolved into a kinder, gentler version, but the 'fear of the afterlife' basics of it all have pretty much remained intact. If you want to escape the fires of hell and get off of this planet alive, you had better make sure you find the correct door, say the right things, believe the right things, and get some good spiritual fruit growing to prove it. In a nutshell, something external out there (pointing up to outer space) needs to be invited to come down and live in here (pointing to my chest). Then, and only then, is our name written in some sort of colossal intergalactic file, known in the book of Revelation as the "Lamb's Book of Life." But here's the important part, the part that you do not want to carelessly miss. If the above procedures and protocols are not followed correctly, you could wind up in a very eternally unfortunate situation.

The Great White Throne Judgment!

Here's the scoop on this according to many preachers: When your heart stops at the end of your gracious life, and you slip peacefully up through those same ceiling tiles your grandpa eased up through, you will find yourself in some sort of Great White Throne Judgment courtroom, where you are the person on trial (basically for the crime of being born a human). It is there where you'll have to 'stand before almighty God' and give an account for what you did, or didn't do in Arizona! Or, at the very least, for what you did or didn't believe. And, if God doesn't see the magic blood, He will point His stern finger at you and say, "Depart from Me! I never even knew you!" There is a reason why this sounds more like something out of the movie *Clash of the Titans* than reality...

For those of you who sincerely feel that I am being disrespectful or off-base here, please stop for a second and consider what I just described. Although uncomfortable to hear, it is in fact what many of us in evangelical circles were taught by well-meaning teachers. Yes, we were. And many churches still teach this today. For centuries, members of the clergy have been visiting those in their last hours, trying their best to dispel the dying person's fears, with 'last rites' prayers and sayings that will hopefully be enough to grant them access through the pearly gates. If we asked nursing home workers how many of their patients are afraid of dying due to religion, we would be appalled. There is something tragically wrong with this, and my heart has always known it.

New Wine Skins?

I was finally beginning to realize that the new wine skins Jesus talked about (as referring to a New Covenant) were not merely about some sort of new and improved religion. It wasn't about moving that old, obligation-based covenant template right over on top of the New Covenant, thus in many ways simply replacing Moses with Jesus. And yet this is precisely what it was beginning to look like many churches had unknowingly done. Using the analogy of new wine skins, Jesus was clearly saying that the old, obligation-based, 'paying God' relationship format wouldn't even fit into the new age's religion-less reality.

Romanticizing our Jesus-only religion and calling it the New Wine Skins doesn't make it the true kingdom any more than putting expensive rims on an old Ford Focus makes it a Ferrari. The New Covenant was never going to be a new improved version of the old covenant. The old was but a mere shadow of the new, and the new was not merely to be an upgraded replica of the old. Someone recently told me, "Ken, if the old covenant was a shadow of the new covenant, then it only stands to reason that it would resemble the old in many ways." You know what? I don't think so.

Shadows on the Lawn

When trying to compare the old covenant with the new covenant, I imagine a beautiful woman and her children dancing in a sun drenched yard accompanied with live music, as they twirl around in a rising sea of floating dandelion seeds. I see how the sun reveals all the colors in their hair. I see the family dog jumping with excitement as if he wants to join in with the festive spirit of the moment. I imagine seeing all of this in slow motion to savor the moment, while listening to the indescribable beauty of their combined laughter and high-pitched screams of joy, all the while contemplating how it makes me feel inside. Then I compare all of that with the dark green, two-dimensional, lifeless shadows on the grass below them. The shadow doesn't even resemble what I just described. How could it? This kingdom, as Jesus called it, just may be deeper and wider and more all-inclusive than we had ever imagined, possibly even more than we are yet fully comfortable with.

What About Sin?

Do we still define sin the same as ancient Judaism does? Is it still a legal matter? Is sin an actual long list of activities that are against the Law of Moses, or is it more of a matter of missing the mark? Could it perhaps be more accurately defined as missing the whole point of life itself? My friend, Jen (my editor), put it this way: "Sin is done. Sin is related to Law. What 'law' do we 'sin' against today, and what is the 'penalty' for 'sinning' against that 'law'? The Law of Moses was never given to us in the first place, so we cannot 'sin' against that Law. Jesus came to 'make an end of sin.'"

Recently a man said to me, "Before Jesus, all we had was the Law." I replied, "When exactly did the Capital Hill area of Seattle have the Law of Moses?" I am not a first-century Jew or Gentile. It is beyond amazing how I had somehow been romantically convinced that I was.

Eckhart Tolle refers to this unfortunate state of mankind as dysfunction or even madness. Hinduism calls it maya. Buddhist writings talk of it as dukkha. Christianity calls it the original sin. I love Eckhart's version of this 'missing the mark,' in his book *A New Earth*. He explains it as living unskillfully and blindly, suffering from the consequence and also causing others to suffer.

Perhaps the original sin was not that Adam ate some forbidden fruit, but that at one point man convinced us that we are all naked and should be ashamed of ourselves for the crime of being human. I do find it interesting how secular law has evolved into an 'innocent until proven guilty' system, whereas the church continues to teach 'guilty until proven innocent.'

What About Repentance?

Is repentance all about 'being sorry' or feeling bad enough? Is it a matter of contrition and genuine sorrowfulness as some sort of penance, or 'heart payment,' or is it simply a matter of turning away from one direction and going in another wiser direction that is more closely aligned with our Source?

What About Forgiveness?

Is forgiveness all about a legal or judicial need for 'absolution' so that we are (legally) in 'right standing with God' and thus 'legally eligible' for both blessings and safe passage into the afterlife? Is forgiveness more for our benefit or more for God, as a requirement to somehow gain or regain His favor or appeasement? Isn't 'forgiveness' more about inner peace from releasing our judgments and ill feelings toward others? Is it about acquittal, or more about renewal?

To me, it was beginning to look like religion in general was about two main things:

1. Paying God.

2. Making sure that you have.

In religion, it seems like it is your job to make God happy (tall order). It is continually romanced as a heart matter but in reality it is a legal, obligation-based matter that is continually being sold as a 'heart matter.'

What About Grace?

What is it? Is it unmerited favor, or proof that no such favor is needed, because it is just as provided as the air we breathe? Is it just another Christian-ese buzzword? I have completely given up on the legal, absolution driven (undeserved) definition at this point. Could it even be scientific in nature? Is it an ancient word, from an ancient religion, about someone else's ancient stuff that has little to do with us? Is that why some have had to define and romance it sixty different ways? Is it humility, gratitude, or some magic-like inner peace? Is it unconditional love and forgiveness for someone who doesn't deserve it? Is that really what grace is? Do we even need to know?

The 'favor' part implies an external being; an outside decision which is a human projection. Being eternally grateful for what you think you don't deserve can be an obstacle in your spiritual walk. It can make you believe there is another debt, the debt of gratitude that could leave you kneeling ever at the cross instead of walking free from it. My friend, Hal, says, "I am curious why so many dear friends hold on to the idea that grace is defined as unmerited favor when old school fundamentalists are the only ones who hold that view, which has been rendered incorrect for years now."

Here are just a few explanations and definitions other people have shared with me:

"The influencing presence of Creator within me ... that aspect of the Divine that continually awakens my thinking to progress, evolve, embrace the 'yet understood' and reflects through me a graciousness towards others."

"Aside from the salvation context (salvation from what since hell is a fable), grace is that which moves you, revealing a deeper identity and mind, surprising you and others around you."

"When you live in a religious paradigm that includes judgment for failure, grace is a very important concept, because it is a contrast from condemnation. Outside of a religious paradigm one realizes that grace is the default position of the One who is our Source. Spiritually aware people understand that our Source doesn't judge, because our Source doesn't need anything, or have any expectations that could be unfulfilled. Our Source is living in and through us; and as such each of us is as perfect and 'holy' as our Source. There isn't any failure."

"Grace is the divine invitation to enjoy unconditional divine love and acceptance while learning to become 'at-one-ment' with the divine I am."

"Grace means influence."

"For me it is a divine influence that creates effortless change as I rest in God."

"Grace, more properly defined, is the divine influence on the heart. We don't earn it (unmerited is a bad word choice that translators have used). But we are all being influenced by the divine all the time."

"Grace is one-way love."

"Grace - Greek evkharisto - means thankfulness, or 'thank you.' We assume it means forgiveness, but I'm not sure if that is correct. Evkharisto is also the word from which we get the term Eucharist. We say grace before a meal to say 'thank you.'"

"I have defined grace as anything that supports you and enables you to move from one moment to the next. Some examples are food, water, air, gravity, and all the physical resources that support our existence. In addition there are things like family, friends, jobs, shelter. These are examples of human resources that support our existence. Then we have things like, love, hope, faith, joy, these are examples of spiritual or emotional resources that support our existence. We do none of these things by ourselves, they are all provided for us, for free; thus, they are grace. Since we could not exist without things like this, a graceless existence is impossible, in this life or the next."

Saying "We need God's grace" is like an ocean fish saying, "We need lots of water" or "If it wasn't for all this salt water." Imagine a tree saying, "I just don't know what I would do without this soil for my roots."

Grace. It's a pretty word, that's for sure, and I think it's okay if we keep using it. Why not? But there are probably several other words that we could use instead, like, "My gosh, this is an amazing, live, breathing, conscious universe that we are a significant part of!" I love what my friend, Diane, had to say about the subject, "I don't know how to define grace. I realize how little I actually do know, and the amazing thing is it's ok. In fact it's better than ok."

What About Obedience and Faithfulness?

Are obedience and faithfulness all about rules and regulations of correctly observing certain laws and commandments, as devotional tasks expected of us by God, or is it simply about eventually comprehending our interactions with Spiritual Law and the benefits of being in closer alignment with our Source? My Christian friend adds, "If we say we live by the Spirit, let us stay in step with the Spirit. We desire to always be 'in agreement' with the Holy Spirit. As Jesus prayed, 'Father, your kingdom come, your will be done in earth as it is in Heaven.'" So is obedience still all about 'obeying' as a legal issue? Or is it not more about recognizing our Source and living in closer harmony with Him?

Another word for "obedience" is "alignment," and another word for "faithfulness" could very well be "synchronicity" in the same fashion that seven musicians are in "obedience" with each other. These are not legal matters as they may have been 'understood' at one time by ancient men, but actually scientific matters having to do more with the promotion and maintenance of life, light, beauty, and love. It is a matter of harmony and symphony and matching vibrational expressions and signatures. Is it possible that the truth about nature is so much grander than we had imagined?

What About Being Born Again?

Is this some sort of born-from-above 'immaculate conception' wherein man somehow becomes a type of science-fiction-like 'host' or 'vessel' for the Spirit of Jesus to come 'live inside' of us, or is it actually a one-time-only interesting choice of words as an analogy-driven term Jesus used in an attempt to explain spiritual enlightenment? Interestingly, Jesus also used the analogy of once again becoming like little children for the same exact subject, suggesting that we would have to return to the nonjudgmental character of an innocent child in order to see, experience, and enter this 'kingdom' of enlightenment, or awakening, or understanding (where all things are spiritually discerned). Is being 'born again' when we telepathically tell a cosmic Jewish religious leader that we accept him as our Master, so he can then remove an evil force from our soul that is present in humanity because a rib-woman was tricked by a talking snake to eat from a magical tree? Is being 'born again' when we say a prayer inviting him to come and live inside of us, where he can now govern and guide our otherwise ungovernable, unguided lives? Did you know that almost every religion on the planet teaches being 'born again,' but simply uses different words? 'Salvation' is also a concept taught by virtually all religions. If another theological philosophy is foreign to us, does that automatically make it wrong?

What About Salvation?

The people of the first century were told of a salvation from physical harm in a 'soon to come' battle with the Roman armies. And yet the apostle Paul also spoke of spiritual growth when he talked of "working out your own salvation."

What if salvation (for us here in the twenty-first century) is not a hopeful mechanism of escape from a tyrannical Creator's sick, twisted, interstellar games for a doomed planet, but rather a door of enlightenment, freedom from our ego-based human nature, and spiritual awakening so we can experience 'heaven' and 'things above' and become all that we were meant to be in the here and now? Is that possible?

Is salvation really about safely getting past some intergalactic gatekeeper of eternity? If we really must insist on using this ancient, *eastern* term, then we ought to use it in its proper, more relevant-to-our-time definition and meaning. 'Salvation' is not exclusive to Christianity or even ancient Judaism. Almost all religions have taught the term as spiritual enlightenment or awakening to something wonderful, not an escape from something terrible. Ancient Buddhist writings talk of 'salvation' as being the 'end of suffering.'

I began to realize that my teachers had conveyed many of these things either wrongly or incompletely, from an old wine skins' format. Perhaps what we are really 'saved' from is ourselves, our own human condition, or egoic, false (carnal) 'self,' to be renewed to know and understand our true (eternal) selves; our true, originating (eternal) life; and thus our true eternal Source. For to know God: this is the actual meaning of 'eternal life.' New and different ways of looking at things are interesting, aren't they?

What Do We Really Know About "Heaven?"

The first definition of "heaven," according to the Christian Bible, is written in Genesis 1:8: "And God called the expanse (*above the waters, from verse 7*) heaven."

So, according to the Bible, God defined "heaven" as the sky.

Throughout the entire Old and New Testaments, we see "heaven" clearly described as the observable sky above us. People are seen looking up towards "heaven," rain falling from "heaven," the stars in the "heavens," someone hearing the voice of God from "heaven," etc. In Psalms 121:1, David writes "I will lift my eyes to the mountains: From whence shall my help come? My help comes from the Lord, who made the heaven and earth."

Is David saying that God may be better accessed by looking up towards the top of Mt. Rainier? Of course not. He is saying that God is 'higher' than us, not that He is higher in 'elevation' than us. In the New Testament, we start noticing that Jesus is talking about a 'kingdom' that is coming, and he tells his first-century audience that this 'kingdom' is actually 'at hand' and very soon to come. It doesn't take us very long to discover that this 'kingdom' is a spiritual kingdom, referred to as the "kingdom of God," and quite frequently the "kingdom of heaven." It is a kingdom that comes "not with observation." He also said that this kingdom was not of this world. Hence, we start getting the idea that heaven is like another dimension that we can 'enter,' or 'see,' or 'live in,' and of course, benefit from. When reading the words of Jesus, it almost sounds like a new age is coming that would enable people to 'see' and actually 'experience' this kingdom being talked so much about.

Then we see the words "Our Father Who art in heaven." Sound confusing?
God names the SKY "heaven" (Gen. 1:8).
"The kingdom of heaven is at hand" (Matt. 3:2).
Jesus is looking toward the sky "heaven" (Matt. 14:19).
We are to be like God Who is in "heaven."
We are told to store up "treasures in heaven" (Matt. 6:19-21).

Are we supposed to believe that in the afterlife, in a physical location called "heaven," we are going to be guided over to a bunch of physical treasures that we have "stored up" for ourselves? Are there actual streets of gold in this heaven? Are there pearly gates? That is just not what the Bible says. In a previous chapter, we have already investigated the subject of the 'New Jerusalem' being a symbolic description of the Bride of Christ (Rev. 21:9; Heb. 12:22-24; I Pet. 2:5). And so, the old church hymn about a "mansion just over the hilltop" with a pearl-filled gate and actual streets of gold is not true (at least not according to the Bible).

Every religion in the world believes in an afterlife (and I do as well), and that an eternal part of 'us' lives on somehow. The Bible actually says that we 'return' to God from where we all came from (Ecclesiastes 12:7). Yet nowhere in the Bible is the title "heaven" given to this afterlife reality.

Two Meanings for the Word "Heaven"

1. The viewable sky above us.

2. Where God 'is.'

God is perfection. God is Love. The fruits of the Spirit are love, joy, peace, patience, kindness, goodness, faithfulness, gentleness, and self-control.

Put Your Minds on "Things Above," Not on "Things Below"

In Colossians 3:2, Paul exhorts us to set our minds on the things "above."

Philippians 4:8 says, "Finally, brethren, whatsoever things are true, whatsoever things are honorable, whatsoever things are just, whatsoever things are pure, whatsoever things are lovely, whatsoever things are of good report; if there be any virtue, and if there be any praise, think on these things."

Both Paul and John talked about dreams and visions, of which some theologians have now decided were descriptions of a physical place, and yet when read in context they obviously describe either something symbolic or someone's attempt to describe either a dream or vision they had. One writer said that to be absent from the body is to be present with the Lord, but not that "heaven" is a physical place where you go when you die. Could it actually be that heaven is not where you go when you die, but where you can 'go' (or be) when you truly live? Could it actually be that eternal life is not that we will live forever, because we already will live forever, but that it is something we can experience and enjoy now, in this life, and in this present realm? Could this present realm actually be the "kingdom of heaven?"

Is it possible that heaven is not physically where God is, but spiritually where God is, and what God is? Jesus came so that we might experience 'God in heaven,' or differently put, "God *and* heaven," right here, right now.

Hence, the "kingdom," and the "King of hearts" (Heb. 10:16).

What is "Eternal Life?"

When are we given an eternal 'soul?' Does God somehow inject each developing human fetus with an eternal soul? Doesn't that sound weird? Doesn't that sound odd and, well, unnatural? Do we really know the answer to that question? Does it happen at the actual second of biological conception, or at the 'age of accountability?' Does it occur when we either accept or reject Jesus as our 'personal Savior,' or as the Jew's Messiah? Or does such an event happen at all? Is the term "eternal life" referring to finally receiving the (legal) right to have a one-way ticket to thankfully being able to 'live forever' with God? Is there really some One monitoring all of that and keeping an actual record book like a scorecard at the bowling alley? Many people claim to know, but does anyone really have all the answers to these questions?

C. S. Lewis once said, "We do not have a soul. We are a soul. What we have is a body."

Many of us have been taught that we are mere mortal, biological units, or human beings who are having a spiritual experience. But what if we are indeed eternal (spiritual) beings having a human experience? And what if "eternal life" is not about where we (someday) go, or someday 'get,' but about whom we (right now) are? Perhaps we are eternal 'lives.' Is that even possible? What if that is what Jesus wanted us to awaken to? Is that such an unreasonable possibility?

When Jesus taught that we would have to return to the innocence of a newborn baby, or become once again "like little children," is it even possible that he could have been saying that we have to go back, to return to a time in our lives when we really knew our true eternal selves? Have we complicated and twisted that into some wild, religious, unrecognizable, spooky, spiritualistic thing? I actually think that is possible.

What if the biblical term "eternal life" was never intended as a time-based phrase – having to do with living 'forever?' What if we already have an 'eternal life,' but many people are not experiencing it or enjoying it, or for that matter, even aware of it? Therefore, some 'have' it, and some don't 'have' it (haven't seen it, or experienced it). What if it is our connectedness to God that Jesus wanted us to awaken to, or to be 'born again' to, where all these things are seen and understood?

You know, to be 'one' with the Father "just as" Jesus was "one with the Father." Does the church have the most accurate-to-reality answers on this? And we know that… how?

What About "Evil" and the "Evil One?"

Some believe that the "devil," interpreted by many also as "Satan," was supposedly an actual being of some sort that at one point in Earth's history was literally "cast down to the earth" from "heaven." If that were true, then wouldn't a simple mission to Mars completely rid us of his influence? We haven't really thought about it like that, have we? Perhaps we should.

At first, I set out to write an entire chapter on this subject, clearly proving how a deeper look at the original language and context of biblical passages throughout the Old and New Testaments reveal that words like "Satan" and "the satan" and "HaSatan" and "satanos" and "diabolos" and "lucifer" and "devil" and "evil one" and "adversary" and "accuser" and "helel" and "star of the morning" and "King of Tyre" and "Beelzebul" (Baalz-zebub: god of Ekron, *Lord of the Flies*) and even "doctrines of demons" (Jewish fables and Greek myths), are all talking about anything but some sort of spooky, invisible being who creeps about the earth trying to steal our joy and lead us astray. For instance, Isaiah speaks metaphorically about the King of Babylon, not an evil angelic being from outer space (Is. 14:12-22). It certainly does not take a Bible scholar to clearly establish this, if one really cares about literary context. There are so many different passages that completely reveal this subject to be something much different than what most of us were taught.

There are so many schools of thought on this subject. To list them all would produce a large book. One thing I can now say with a great deal of personal confidence is that when we are reading those ancient Middle Eastern documents, we are attempting to comprehend a richly flavored language that, if we could be honest with ourselves, we know almost nothing about.

When I Lived with Monsters and Angels

I was raised in a land with monsters and angels. There was a reason to be afraid of the dark, because something evil was … 'out there', always watching, always keeping track of your behavior, and looking for the slightest sign of spiritual weakness. It was … *the devil*, and his main goal was to somehow cause you to disappoint your "heavenly Father", thus placing you in a state of shame. He was the 'accuser of the brethren'… "Look what you've done, you rotten sinner!" he would say, as he laughed under his breath at you for falling into his well-orchestrated traps. As if that wasn't bad enough, we also had the Holy Spirit basically agreeing with him, adding to the mix something called, "holy conviction"/guilt, designed to draw you to repentance and thus restoration, of course. At least that was what we were being taught.

Imagine a battlefield set up somewhat like a football field, the fifty yard line being a sharp, solid dividing line between good and evil. It was like growing up on the set of Harry Potter, and (sincerely) believing that it is not a movie. You were either working for the evil one or working for the Lord. The devil, also known as Satan, was your constant opponent. God, of course (along with the pastor), was always trying to offer you more powerful weaponry to triumph over this evil monster. Everything was a battle, and every day was seen as being on the battle field… Hence the old saying, "How goes the battle?" Many of life's every day, ordinary challenges were seen as "fiery darts of the devil", you know, trying to defeat you, or at the very least, steal your joy. The reason this stealthy being had so much interest in you is because he was sore at God for casting him down to the planet earth. Therefore, he had made it his life's mission to destroy the lives of as many humans as possible. That was the church's story anyway, and the last time I checked – they're sticking to it. We were assured that if we remained faithful to God by 'living holy lives', staying 'in His Word', and spending plenty of time in prayer, He would assist and support us on this … war zone of life. I often wondered why God and the devil couldn't just go somewhere and settle this score without us. And wouldn't that make more sense?

The term "backslidden" never really carried much psychological weight for me, but the "fence" scenario did. I remember many a sermon explaining how no one is "on the fence". You were either on this side of the fence, or on the other side. You were either making God happy, very happy, extremely proud, or you were making Him sad, very sad, or extremely grieved. This church world was a mythological and magical place where God and His angels were continually doing their best to influence you toward good, and the devil with his demons were trying to influence you toward evil. And so, somewhere ... out there, the forces that be were pulling you back and forth, like a tug of war, each side wanting your soul as their reward. I guess that should make us feel important to both sides, if only I still believed that movie-worthy version of reality. It was not a world built around the importance of psychological wellness or personal growth, but one of spiritual and physical safety, and something called "Christian growth".

The Bible was a magic book from which one could obtain even greater power over the forces of darkness. It provided stronger, protective armor in this invisible conflict that was continually raging in the wind that blew through the maples in the front yard and around the east side of the house. Ironically, we thought ancient, uncivilized tribes in South American rainforests were silly for dancing around the perimeters of their dwellings, shaking things while chanting memorized sayings from their ancestors. And yet without even knowing it, we were doing the same exact thing. But we weren't using the ancient words from our own ancestors, but from someone else's ancestors of a completely different ancient Middle Eastern culture, of which we honestly knew very little about.

Is Evil Real?

I think that most people, including myself, would have to say, "Yes." A friend of mine recently said that the 'evil one' is a metaphor dealing with our human ego, or our carnal nature that is in conflict with our true eternal selves. So, basically what he was saying is that we have located the enemy, and it is us. Obviously, humans are capable of living and operating at extremely low vibrational levels, making very poor choices, and doing very dark things. Some say that sin, evil, sickness, and even disease are all inventions (or manifested creations) of man. I believe that mankind possesses unimaginable power to overcome these sorts of things and eventually completely eradicate such inventions and their manifestations as well. Yes, I actually do believe that the human race will evolve spiritually to the extent of one day making evil (however it came about) disappear completely. It might be five hundred years from now, or it might not be for five thousand years, but I truly do believe it is our ultimate destiny.

Unexplainable Darkness

Many of us have all heard first-hand stories of people who have personally witnessed evil activity including what they call 'demon possession.' I would not discount those experiences, but what I find very peculiar is if you want to see such things, your best bet is to hang out with some local Pentecostals. Not only would you have better luck running into such things in Pentecostal or Charismatic circles than your local tavern or crack house, but the entire first-century church record is sorely lacking of such occurrences as well. I can really relate to what Pastor Don Keathley (from gracepointnetwork.com) said, "Note to my charismatic brothers: When you stop fighting the devil, you will discover that he doesn't show up anymore."

But what about the demon possessed people talked about during the time of Jesus? When was the last time you heard on the local news that the police in downtown Seattle are now in a standoff with a demon-possessed man? Not lately, right? But on an almost daily basis, the police of every large city in our nation do deal with people proven to have mental health problems. In the days of the Bible, those who had the horrible disease of leprosy were called 'unclean' and forced to live outside the city walls (and not just for health reasons). Others thought they were cursed either because of something they did or something their parents did. Today we treat such people with modern medicine, and after recovering fully they end up becoming airline pilots, doctors, and schoolteachers. We do the same for the chronically depressed and people suffering from mental disorders. Regardless of how low or deep a person can venture into the dark unknown, I am convinced that such occurrences have more to do with the person involved than some sort of extra-terrestrial, invisible monster uninvitingly taking possession of someone's life.

Listen to the brilliant words of Uell S. Anderson: "Let us sensibly get rid of both the devil and hell. Make up your mind that the intelligence behind the universe does not destroy itself! The pain-ridden idea of hellfire as a place of punishment for sin is man's own morbid idea; evil is man's own morbid idea; disease and suffering are man's own morbid ideas. Since God created man free, He has left it up to man to conceive his own situations. And man has thought into existence all evil!"

An extremely helpful study on this subject is the website called realdevil.info.

Jesus in Our Box?

Question: How much of what Jesus said is first-century specific, or first-century Jewish specific, or even first-century event specific? Which verses and passages are metaphorical, symbolic, or analogy-driven, and which ones are to be viewed as literal, or global?

There is much about those ancient Middle Eastern religious writings we still do not fully understand. Not only was Jerusalem a melting pot and huge commerce center in the first century, but, as previously mentioned, it was also richly influenced by ancient Roman, Greek, Asian, and certainly Egyptian culture. Even their normal military battles were written out like an episode right out of the pages of *Jason and the Argonauts*. Much poetry and earth-shaking mythological language was used in those ancient cultures to describe both events and concepts so as to render them with great importance. To deny this common literary practice being employed all throughout the Bible is to be intellectually dishonest in my opinion.

There are many places in the New Testament where Jesus and the apostles make statements of which you and I would jump in and say, "What?! Please explain that!" but the original audience remains seated, you know, as if what was just said made perfect (common) sense to them. Have we not taken those ancient passages, literalized some, globalized some, futurized others, westernized and re-culturized most of them? Is it even possible that many of our current interpretations are yet to be revealed as incorrect and almost opposite in some cases of their original intent?

What is Truth?

"If you would be a real seeker after truth, it is necessary that at least once in your life you doubt, as far as possible, all things." - Rene Descartes (1596-1650)

I hope you are enjoying reading this book of questions as much as I enjoyed writing it. When we are finally free from any fear of questioning the old answers, with nothing to lose and everything to gain, life becomes an adventurous voyage of exploration into our potential. As you may have noticed, even some of the discoveries at the front of this book were also now beginning to come into question and re-evaluation for me. When we begin to connect some of the newly-introduced dots of truth, some of the old dots we were once so sure about start becoming unconnected. A close family member recently told me, "Ken! It seems like every time we talk, you believe something new!" I thought to myself, "But wait... isn't that how it is supposed to be? Isn't life about growing and evolving into greater understanding? And isn't a part of that a process of having to let go of old things we were once so sure about?"

There is one thing that truth produces more than anything else, and that is freedom. There is one thing that truth destroys more than anything else, and that is fear. In many religious circles, the acquisition of truth has been mystified as if it were something one could only obtain through deeply devotional means of some illusive, magic like impartation, or having been chosen to discover some otherwise unseen, deeper truth that those around you have not yet found. This confounded, enchanted idea of truth makes me think of some science fiction fantasy wherein one must climb a mountain, unlock twelve coded keys with hidden words in some ancient book, enter the cave of the dragon, and look directly into his left eye. Then and only then will you be granted the vision of the sword, etc. But what if truth is simply defined as "the way things really are here, and the way things really work here"? What if it is not mystical or illusive, or hidden, or for sale, or only obtained by doing the right things or believing the right things? What if it never was? What if it is as free as the water in a nearby river?

Truth that changes minor details in our ideology is fine and sometimes even welcomed, but truth that changes our everything? Well, it's just not truth, period. We won't accept it, we won't entertain it, we won't seriously investigate it, and we won't believe it. We know better, and that's that. As a Christian, I was taught that any truth outside of our church's doctrines was not truth, but deceptive and sinister counterfeits of truth. Looking back, this hauntingly resembles the movie *The Village*, directed by M. Night Shyamalan, where young people were kept safely away from the rest of society by a well-meaning older generation who wanted to shelter them from the evil world outside the camp, only to find that it wasn't an evil world, but just reality.

I was taught from a very early age to look at other religions as sorely incomplete and even dangerously misleading, and that we Christians were the only group who had somehow captured universal truth. Other religions, even if they had so many paralleling truths with Christianity, were viewed as either having stolen those truths from the Bible or they just accidentally stumbled onto some of our truths. New Age and New Thought authors were thought of as downright dangerous and dark as hell itself. We were to be very leery of those wicked Eastern religions, but Middle Eastern religions? Um, not so much. Even the Zodiac place mats at the Chinese restaurants were quickly turned upside down by some of the Christians I grew up with.

The Fallacy of Truth Ownership

Many times in life when we first hear newly-revealed truth, rather than saying, "Wow! That's awesome!", we become insulted instead. There comes a time in all our lives when we realize that the answers and explanations for some of the deeper questions in life actually are found outside of our particular inherited belief system. At that point, rather than humbly investigating the possibility of our doctrines needing a serious upgrade from an outside source, most of us just stop asking those kinds of questions, carelessly filling in those awkward spaces with trivial matters, distractive toys, recreation, and entertainment.

Can we be honest with ourselves? When the answers we are inquisitive about begin to clearly reveal themselves as contrary in any way to what we have been taught, we quickly abandon the questions, rather than compromising our solidly established belief systems. It is so much easier believing in someone else's interpretations of truth, because that way we never have to really think for ourselves. We don't have to reason things out. We don't have to consider all the facts, and we don't have to have our lives uncomfortably interrupted by newly discovered truths that sharply challenge our old truths. When we say we like being philosophically challenged, we don't mean that we like our established truth challenged. What we really mean is that we like having our established truth re-confirmed as the fullest possible truth, and for the most part, only by the people we agree with. Therefore, we don't study or seriously investigate the things we really don't want to be true.

We all want to believe that the truth is somehow trapped within only one particular religion, but when we decide that is the way things are, our religion becomes ideology, creating an illusory sense of superiority, which soon creates division and conflict between us and our fellow man. Religious teachings have always been signposts, or maps, or clues to help us in our quest for spiritual growth.

Pointing to the Moon (Inspired from Ancient Buddhist Text)

Pointing at the moon with your finger is not the moon. Your pointing is not the moon, nor is your finger the moon. Just as a map of Florida is not Florida, the words on a page in a book may be about the truth, pointing to or toward the truth, but are not the truth itself. Can the truth be put into words? Yes, but the words are, of course, not it. They only point to it.

Imagine if you woke up one morning and found that much of what you've been taught about God, life, nature, spirituality, and even yourself have been more of a collection of analogies and metaphors that point to the real story. What if many of the ways in which we were taught to look at the teachings of Jesus are actually incorrect? Could we handle that? Would we have the ability to accept that if it were actually shown to us? Or would we fight like good Christian soldiers against such truth? Imagine studying a boat for forty years only to find out that all this time you were actually studying a bus. Such is the story of many, including myself.

Is Jesus the Only Way to God?

Whenever you ask, "What is truth?" someone will shout out "Jesus is the truth." They will also quote the verse in which Jesus tells his disciples, "No one comes to the Father but through me" (John 14:6). But what does that mean? Does that really mean that no one can find or experience God unless they convert to Christianity? Is that really what Jesus was saying? Was he really starting a brand new 'Jesus-only' religion?

There are actually other interpretations of this passage that I was not aware of. Was Jesus merely having a small group directed teacher/student conversation about how they were to follow his mentoring only and not the instructions of any other teacher, or was this really some sort of global, State of the Union Address to all of humanity, of how no person on the face of the earth throughout all of human history will be able to access God or an eternal afterlife without going 'through Jesus' first? Interestingly, there is an abundant supply of testimonies from every single religion on the planet of answered prayers and miracles, and most of them don't go through Jesus to get to God. But how is that possible if indeed no one can get to the Father without becoming a Christian? Is this truly a legal matter of mandatory procedures and protocols? Did you know that Siddhartha Gautama told his disciples almost exactly the same thing, word for word? Does that mean that anyone born in Japan must go through Buddhism to get to God?

The Tacoma Narrows Bridge

There's a toll bridge not far from my home that spans a part of the Puget Sound. If you drive up to the booth and say, "I want to go across but I have no money. How can I go across?" The toll lady will say, "No one goes to Tacoma but through me." But is that really true? Yes, it is if you are on that particular road, sitting with your car parked next to that toll booth, and have decided that this bridge is how you wish to get to Tacoma. By the driver's choice of pulling up to that toll booth, he is saying, "I want to get to Tacoma by going through you."

In the same way, if the disciples had made their decision to get to God through the teachings of Jesus, then as their teacher, he could very well have been using the same conversational construct as the toll booth lady. Why would that be such an unreasonable interpretation of this verse? Is it possible that we have taken an ancient conversation and built it into some sort of spooky, weird, intergalactic gate keeper to the afterlife protocol one must strictly observe in order to obtain a proper, validated ticket to making it out of here alive? Is our 'convert or die' religion, that we don't like to admit we believe in, precisely what we have been talked into believing? Some of course will romance this by saying, 'convert to live' and have life more abundantly, and that is beautiful; but without saying it, they are also saying 'or else,' are they not?

The Uninformed Eskimo

There's a story about an old Eskimo and a Christian missionary. The Eskimo asks, "If I did not know about your God, or sin, or this man you call Jesus, would I go to hell?" The missionary answers him, "No. Not if you were never told of such things." The Eskimo then scratches his head and replies, "Then why did you tell me?"

And what about the ancient Siberians or folks in northern China or the Aborigines who lived out their entire lives without ever hearing of Jesus or the gospel? These are uncomfortable questions, are they not? I think our hearts have always known the answers to these questions.

The Man or the Message?

Was Jesus not speaking about the love that he is, or the message, or the embodiment of what he is? Or was he (literally) presenting himself as some sort of magic door, as the man from Galilee that we all must 'go through?'

Could it be that love is the way, the truth, and the life? Jesus was all about Spirit and life and showing us that within each man. Have we gotten hung up on the *man* Jesus, not realizing that he was pointing us to the Christ (spirit, or Christ consciousness) within all of us? Although such concepts and terminologies are foreign to us, does that automatically render them incorrect?

Fundamental Christians often quote John 14:6 in support of the false doctrine of eternal punishment in hell. In fact, they would say that this verse, like the rest of the Bible, needs no interpretation -- just accept what it clearly says. Jews call The Torah "The Way." Here's a prayer that Jews always pray before reading The Torah: "Thank you, O Lord, for giving us The Torah of truth which sets before us the way of everlasting life." So there you have it: the way, the truth, and the life. Perhaps the deeper truth, not the superficial, is that Jesus was saying that He was the embodiment of The Torah. A rabbi being seen or expressed as the embodiment of the Torah would have been a common understanding among Jews. In John 5:39 we read, "Search the scriptures ... for they testify of me." "The scriptures" would be The Torah since, when Jesus spoke these words, the New Testament was not yet written. Was he setting forth a new exclusive way to God that would result in the eternal damnation of the vast majority of the human race, all of whom he died to save? Or was Jesus saying that people come to God through the whole truth of the word of God in The Torah?

My buddy Scott, from San Diego shared this.

> My view is that any enlightened master (Jesus, Buddha, etc.) has an altruistic and fundamental understanding of selflessness, and they embody individuality without a belief in self. Leaving aside how 'the Father' might be understood we are left with 'no one gets to the Father except through me'. Literalists, as we see in common Christendom, apply their contextual modes of thought and see 'believe/faith in Jesus' as they have been trained to see. I, however, am of the opinion to inquire deeper into how a selfless (literally no self-view inside them) being can make such a seemingly egocentric statement (i.e. 'me').

Contextually speaking the question was asked: 'What is the way?' Jesus pointed to his life as an answer; please continue refraining from literal modes of thought. Jesus was not pointing to his methodologies or works, but a state of being. He repeatedly told his disciples they already 'knew' (after they asked and clearly stated 'we don't know') and, once again, pointed to himself. Are you yet seeing the nature of my inquiry?

If we attempt to apply a literalist point of view, we will conceptualize an individual and label it 'Jesus,' especially if the way is 'through' Jesus. Such literalized thinking is condition based and will remain from the vantage point of the person's sense of 'self,' yet we are discussing enlightened masters who consistently abandon the belief of self. This approach is fundamentally unsuited. This must be approached from the understanding that Jesus was not pointing to individuality (himself).

In John 14:6 Jesus said: "I am the way to, and the truth, and the life; no one comes to the Father but through me". First understand that "truth" means reality and life means fullness (think supreme tranquility). Earlier in context of this chapter Jesus stated, "you know the way". Jesus was confident in that his friends had experienced him enough to know the way. 'What is the way then?!' you are probably asking. Aside from parables and idioms, it is not laid out in what or how Jesus realized salvation. What we see in this passage (story) was his confidence in his friends' experience to know. He also understood his salvation as synonymous for their own, which we see in the language Saint Paul uses of "co-crucified" and "co-resurrected". He was not laying out a blanket statement of faith as we have been taught; he was speaking as a friend to friends who were in one another's daily lives.

Charlie, from Bedford, New Hampshire gives these very enlightening thoughts.

There is the whole Jewish dialect and style of linguistics and hyperbole, all of which is not taken into account in church theology and in the modern western view of how to understand the verses. The earliest of writings indicate that when Jesus said, 'No one comes to the Father but through me,' in the linguistics of the time, it would be more appropriate for this verse to be translated, 'No one comes to the Father but by doing what I do.' So then the question bears, what was Jesus doing that causes him to be close to the father? The answer to that is what being a Christian is about, not the Christian requirements put forth to obtaining eternal unconditional love. It always strikes me as sad/funny that God has unconditional love but conditions must be met to know the unconditional love. Christian theology has twisted what the word *"unconditional"* means by definition. The mainstream Christian God is not unconditional and that's a fact, there are too many caveats to God's unconditional love according to the Christian theology. Essentially, the proper translation is, you will know God if you do what I do, that is of course, to *love*.

Quantum Physics shows us scientifically that *all* energy is the same energy just taking different mass forms. Since this is the factual case, then it would mean that *all* energy of the soul is the same energy. Jesus, in Matthew, went on and on about being *one* with the Father and the disciples, and that the disciples and people in general are *one* with the Father. Buddha also said the same, oddly. All the masters have said the same thing: that we are *one* with one another and to the 'God' energy. *If* that is the case, then there is no hierarchy. No one will be the 'winner' Messiah while others pay tribute. No, in fact, what it will be is pure perfect union with all. Heaven is not set up like it is here on earth. There are no 'have and have nots' to any measure. One is not 'closer' to God while another is further away. Jesus carries no deeper kinship with God than I do, so the first sin is the belief that there is separation. The 'salvation' is to realize this lie. Thankfully, Quantum Physics science is not only supporting the deeper spiritual knowledge presented by Jesus and other masters *but* is also making fools of those who think there is a separate entity, which, of course, is just a façade. The fact of the matter is we are all from the same energy source and will return to the same energy source.

Oh, and 'the way' to heaven/God is through no one other than ourselves: no historical or religious figure. Jesus, Buddha, or whoever might point to a path, but you choose to walk it. No master walks the path for you; the 'way' is through the self. When we are honest, we acknowledge that we are fully responsible for how the path is walked, whether we choose to follow a creed someone told us about or make up our own religious doctrine. The bottom line is, we, the individuals, pick and choose. Everything emanates from our own point of view and hearts. In reality, even if we take on the disguise of a religion, we indeed create our own 'salvation,' and create our own path to God.

Let me flesh it out another way. 'Love does not show favorites.' Most Christians would agree with that statement when they think of love in its highest form. Although most of us do not flesh out the definition of love to its fullest, when we do, we discover a different theology. If love does not show favorites in its highest form, this would mean that love's fullest embrace (presumably for most of us, after we physically die) would show no favorites. God, the embodiment of love, would show no favorites. This means that Jesus does not hold a more 'favorite' place than Buddha or any other soul in the eyes of God, and likewise, the individual soul who is made in the image of God, that is *love*. We would not hold Jesus, or any other, even God, at a higher 'favorite' standing above any other. My love for God would be equal to my love for Ken Dahl; there would be no difference. This is the 'oneness' that Jesus is talking about when fully fleshed out to its logical 'end.'

So to that end, the idea that the only way to Heaven is through Jesus loses all merit because at the core of the Christian message is love, and love does not show favoritism. Is this path narrow? Yes. Many do not choose to live in love to the fullest extent possible in the human realm and they 'miss' the opportunity to have God/love as a living presence in their lives. The belief in separation, not being inside love, is an experienced hell on earth.

The 'Christ' of all religions teaches that love is the key. When we as individuals choose love (Buddhists call it compassion) and view it theologically to its fullest measure, the 'way,' the 'path,' becomes crystal clear. The way to God is by love, not by measured steps or works. Mainstream Christianity has disguised 'works' as 'faith' in becoming 'saved.' Love shows no favorites, therefore, God does not favor the 'saved by Jesus' more than those not 'saved by Jesus.' For to do so would be a heavenly love that shows favorites, adheres to a hierarchy, a holy love that believes in human made construct of 'worthy and worthless.' Not at any point is the love of God to any human ever worthless and thrown out. Love enables all paths to God. *If* love did not, then it would cease to be love at its fullest fleshed out definition.

Ariel, from London, Ontario says:

The use of the word 'father' is a metaphor, or truth-pointer to an inexpressible phenomenon … so then everyone's distillation of the message will be personal. What if he was saying, "Find the essence of you, as I have found the essence of me, and don't be afraid, because it is in you, as much as it is in me? What if one gets to the father by finding the 'I am' in ourselves, that Jesus found in himself, a sometimes dormant potential, or unrecognized inherent value? What if this is a reminder that, as Jesus is human and found the Father, that we are human and can also find the Father in us? What if Jesus didn't come to give us the spirit, but to remind us that we always had it? What if Jesus didn't come to forgive us our sins, but to remind us that we always were and always are forgiven? What if the only thing obscuring the *love* that we all are is the egotistical belief that we are sinners, can't experience truth, can't be love apart from Jesus? What if we all are 'the way, the truth, and the life' and just haven't seen/experienced/proven it to ourselves yet? Under what authority do we presume to hide under our bushel baskets? And why do we proclaim ourselves to be in darkness, when we could just as easily be blinded to the *love* that we are?

> If you are not the light, then who convinced you that you were darkness? Who told you that you were naked, when you're so beautifully resplendent as love's image and fullness, unadorned?

Bruce, from Taylorsville, North Carolina:

> Love, pure and simple, is the *life* that speaks Life to everything and is the Life of everything. It was *love* speaking through a clear transparent vessel without any interference. When found and experienced, *love* is the testimony: the Way, the Truth, and the Life, of all.

And so, as you can see, there are several ways of looking at these old, familiar passages. A vivid definition of "religion" is "trustingly believing that the old information is all the information (and is the completely formulated, correctly processed, perfectly understood, beyond questioning interpretation)." You know, like believing that our generation is pretty much the generation that finally has the Bible all figured out.

Five

WHAT ABOUT BIBLE INERRANCY?

Is the Christian Bible an amazing book? Absolutely! It is actually way beyond amazing and without argument the most significant collection of ancient religious and spiritual writings in all of human history. But is it inerrant, meaning without contradiction? Are we willing to question such things? Are we unafraid and actually able to look directly at the uncomfortable facts, allowing them to be what they are? Is that us? Or are there 'just some things' that are off limits for logic and deductive reasoning?

How We've Been Taught to View the Bible

If we are to be nakedly honest with ourselves, Bible reading, over time, has evolved into somewhat of a fear-based occupation. Although we do love the wonderful life-changing truths within its pages, many of us have been trained with the subconscious approach of over-analyzing it as if it were some sort of extra-terrestrial document that was somehow hand delivered by God Himself. We see it like something out of the movie *The Scorpion King* or *Raiders of the Lost Ark*, in which every sentence, comma, and word is somehow a gear or cogged key

WHAT ABOUT BIBLE INERRANCY?

that unlocks the next perfect clicker, in some massively intricate, tumbler-driven bank door, that leads to the other codes and keys, that when all perfectly fitted together, finally reveals the seamless, unadulterated truth of all truths. The world looks at this mystical, 'God authored' mindset with more than a raised eyebrow, as they should. We have done this for so long that we can't even see just how bizarre it really is.

Jesus once said, "You search the scriptures, for in them you think you have eternal life; and these are they which testify of me." He also called the Pharisees "snakes and vipers," yet they knew the scriptures better than anyone.

My friend, Paul, wrote this:

> For many believers, the Bible (not Jesus) is the most holy authority there is. They would never say this, but how their faith functions is not always how it is admitted and professed. I suspect that for many Christians, despite what they say, God actually seems far off, Christ is a great idea, Person, and Savior, but what seems most real, most accessible, most reliable (and unfortunately, most controllable) is the Bible.

With a fine-toothed comb, we "search the scriptures" with this multi-faceted, puzzle like, obligation-based dissection, making sure to check both the Hebrew and Greek, in the hopes that we haven't dangerously missed some eternally consequential text. Even though we have been trained to actually study the Bible as a sort of 'Great Big Magic Puzzle Book,' is that really what it is? Have our theologians not in fact turned the teachings of Jesus into the most confusing, contradictory, theologically schizophrenic religion on the planet? Or are they 'spot on' with their 'scripture must interpret scripture' grand hermeneutical formulas? Many people, including myself, are beginning to seriously question this, and for well thought out, intelligent reasons. Was the Bible literally God-dictated, or written by mere men who were simply doing the best they could in trying to explain their experiences with the unexplainable, and therefore their concepts as well?

Now Start Studying!

Imagine God being in the delivery room when you were born, and He says to you, "Hey there, little guy! Welcome to my planet full of beautiful lakes and oceans and flowers and mountains and meadows and music and art and delicious fruit and romance and love and joy and marriage and parenthood. *NOW START STUDYING!!!*"

The reason that is hard for us to imagine is because there is no such demonstrative, demanding character in reality, only in religion.

The History Behind the Bible

Growing up in the church, I was taught very little about the actual history behind the Bible and how it all came together. I never knew that all those ancient, cherry-picked documents eventually got put together after editing, being debated on, voted on, and even after removing dozens of books (including several 'gospels'), to then finally become what we know today as the 'Bible.' All evangelical churches claim to be vehemently against adding to or taking away from the Bible, and yet the leaders of these same institutions don't seem to mind at all that fourth and fifth-century Roman church leaders and transcribers did exactly that. One fellow justified all that foul play by saying, "There were good reasons all that stuff got left out." But who is to judge that? What is such blind trust from parishioners based upon? Do we just carelessly say, "Oh, those really smart early church fathers knew what they were doing"? Are we to conclude that God also directed the hands of the early Catholic priests and translators in Rome? When we really start investigating these matters, we quickly learn that there is much more to this story than most of us have been told.

Is the Christian Bible that many call the "Word of God" the actual God-dictated 'sentence by sentence' words of God Himself? Many people believe it is. In this section, I would like to fearlessly question this as well as showcase the many responses I have received for such 'irreverent' questioning. The main verse used to support inerrancy is 2 Timothy 3:16-17: "All Scripture is inspired by

God." Interestingly, we seldom hear any emphasis on the prior verse, 3:15, which reveals how Paul was ironically referring only to the Old Testament scriptures (The Torah). There was no such thing as New Testament scriptures at that time.

Many have been taught to view the Bible in its current form as the perfectly assembled, complete collection of God-directed documents. Some believe that the very sentence structure of every single verse is the precise, intended expression of God Himself. One would think that an Intelligence that can create five hundred billion other galaxies could also write a book without inconsistencies, blatant contradictions, and a history of obvious foul play of leaving out entire chapters while adding questionable text decades later, and in some cases centuries later. For example, very few Christians know (what virtually all serious scholars now uncomfortably admit) that the ascension texts and the virgin birth texts were both added as late as nine decades (90 years) after the earliest known manuscripts - where both of these subjects did not exist. Nor are most Christians aware that the original text of Isaiah 7:14 never did have the word "virgin" in it, but merely says, "a woman is with child," and yet in most of today's leading Bibles, it does contain the word "virgin." I had no idea that the story in the epistle of John about the woman caught in adultery was actually added hundreds of years after the first, most well-known manuscripts of this letter. Did you know that? Did you know that this is all common knowledge among theologians and Bible scholars? Yet who among us have ever heard of these things from our pastors?

I am not even scratching the surface here on credible, verifiable information that is available for anyone to research for themselves. Why am I showing you these things? Because they are truth, and they tell us things that change the way in which we look at the Bible. Should we not want to know about these things?

The Books of the Old Testament

I had no idea that the books of the Old Testament are the end result of an eventual merging of three different collections of documents from different kingdoms. I did not know that Moses could very well be a composite of several different people. Most Christians do not know that several 600-year-old writings attributed to Moses were actually discovered during the renovation of the Temple in the Southern Kingdom called "Judah." The first sentence of the Old Testament was not written down until almost forty-five generations after the life of Abraham (900 years later). Virtually all of the stories involving Moses, including the giving of the Law at Mount Sinai, were passed down orally through fifteen generations after the death of Moses himself, before they were ever written down. Also, did you know that the first five books of the Old Testament (Pentateuch) were probably not written by Moses, but by several authors and then weaved into one document hundreds of years later? I did not know that. Have you ever heard of "Gaf and Wellhausen"? Do you remember any preacher ever explaining the differences of origin, authorship, significance, and application of the Yahwist documents, the Elohist documents, the Deuteronomic writings, or the Priestly documents? Did you know that the blending together of all these separate writings had more to do with ancient Jewish politics and war than divine guidance? I am honestly not asking these questions to sound 'learned.' I am just now finding out for myself that these are indeed fundamental level considerations about the history of the Bible that we all should have been taught about if unprotected truth were really the goal of theologians.

Was the war between first-century Rome and Jerusalem really about the Creator of the universe bringing judgment upon Jerusalem, or was it just another war in the history of mankind, recorded from the perspective of some ancient religious sect?

The Genesis Account

In Genesis, God creates light and separates light from darkness, and day from night, on the first day. Yet He did not make the light producing objects (sun, moon, and stars) until the fourth day. Plants are made on the third day before there was a sun to drive their photosynthetic processes. Also, if God created the sun on the fourth day, how had four days passed?

"He made the stars also." God spends a day making light (before making the stars) and separating light from darkness; then almost as an afterthought, he makes the trillions of stars (Gen. 1:16). "And God set them in the firmament of the heaven to give light upon the earth." Really? Then why are only a tiny fraction of stars visible from earth, not to mention 300 to 500 billion other galaxies that are full of their own billions of stars and solar systems. Yet this verse says that God put the stars in the firmament "to give light" to the earth (1:17).

And so, what we have here is a creation 'story' that sharply contradicts the very laws of nature that God was supposedly creating. For many, such questions of course fall under the 'unimportant truths' category. God curses the serpent. From now on the serpent will crawl on his belly and eat dust. But how did this snake get around before?

How could you have a preconceived notion of 'morning' before the sun was created? Read what one of the Patriarchs of Christianity said about the creation story in AD 230:

> Now what man of intelligence will believe that the first and the second and the third day, and the evening and the morning existed without the sun and the moon and the stars? And that the first day, if we may so call it, was even without a heaven? And who is so silly as to believe that God, after the manner of a farmer, planted a paradise eastward in Eden, and set in it a visible and palpable tree of life, of such a sort that anyone who tasted its fruit with his bodily teeth would gain life; and again that one could partake of good and evil by masticating the fruit taken from the tree of that name? ... I do not think that anyone will doubt that these are figurative expressions which indicate certain mysteries through a semblance of history and not through actual events. - Origen, De Principiis, IV.3.1, Philocalia, I.17.

Did you know that the creation story of the Bible was actually modeled after an ancient Babylonian story? The writers of Genesis (the Jewish version) wrote that it all took place in a six day period so that God could be seen as resting on the seventh day. Most Christians are also unaware of the fact that the revised Jewish version was not about an explanation of how the physical world was made, but about the Sabbath being established as a defining mark of true Judaism.

At one point in the Bible, God supposedly 'stops' the sun from going down so that the Jewish army can kill more people (Josh. 10:1-15). Unfortunately stopping the sun would not accommodate that need, but stopping the earth from spinning would. In Ecclesiastes 1:5, it reads, "The sun rises and the sun sets, and hurries back to where it rises." This was one of the stronger verses the Catholic Church used against Galileo's 'blasphemy' (1633) of asserting that the earth is orbiting the sun.

"Ken, Why Are You Doing This? Where Is the Love?"

Such innocent and reasonable questions have produced everything from deeply saddened readers, to disrespectful insults and name calling, to the most wild, irrational explanations imaginable. These unfavorable responses only fueled more questions for me. The rationale among many of my peers seemed to be, "If we don't want to believe that the Bible has any literary inconsistencies or contradictions, then it doesn't." In other words, "Everything in the Bible is true because the Bible says it is true." After doing some deeper study and historical research, it was encouraging to learn that many renowned Bible scholars now also believe it is a real possibility that the creation story, along with several other stories, are exactly that: stories.

One doesn't have to do a whole lot of research to confirm that there were many different civilizations here, and in many parts of the globe, long before the supposed era of Adam and Eve (5000 BCE). Other civilizations as early as 12,000 BCE on the opposite side of the planet have been solidly confirmed. There are hundreds of pyramids around the globe, many of which pre-date 5000 BCE, and many of which have yet to be unearthed. There are human rock carvings here in America dating around 14,800 years old. Skeletal remains of humans predating even those numbers have been found. The amount of evidence for an earth that is countless millions of years old is beyond overwhelming. If a person is willing to do the research, they will find all this credible information, and so much more. But again, we usually don't search for what we don't really want to find. It is not so much a matter of believing or not believing the Bible. It is about understanding that we have just obediently accepted it as something much different than it historically is. Consequently, when one does their thorough homework on its history, one ends up walking away, not with less appreciation for it, but more.

The Four Gospels

Many world-renowned Bible scholars have arrived at the position that the authors of these four documents are almost certainly not the actual authors named in our Bibles. The followers of Jesus were uneducated, Aramaic speaking peasants from the area of Galilee (Acts 4:13). These gospels were not only written in Greek, but the authors were highly educated in above average Greek composition.

Stories that are passed down orally for years obviously lose some of their original integrity. In the book of Mark, Jesus is crucified after the Passover meal, but in the book of John, before the meal. According to Mark, Jesus died early in the morning, but John says, not until late afternoon. There are several other differentiations between these four documents as well: Did Judas betray Jesus for money, or because "Satan entered him," or because Jesus told him to? Did he hang himself, or did he fall upon something that tore open his stomach? Did Jesus carry his cross the entire way to the crucifixion site, or did Simon? The answers to these questions depend on which gospel you are looking at. Did one of the thieves mock Jesus, or both? Did the curtain in the temple rip after the death of Jesus, or before? Did Mary go to the tomb alone, or with others? Was the stone removed before they arrived at the tomb, or not? What did they see when they arrived: one man, two men, or an angel? Were Mary and the other women told to tell the disciples to stay in Jerusalem, or were they to go directly to Galilee? Did the disciples leave Jerusalem, or did they go to Galilee? If one reads these four accounts side-by-side, one clearly discovers something quite troubling. Also quite interesting is how no preacher ever addresses the odd passages surrounding the crucifixion; like Mary Magdalene talking to a man who she thinks is the graveyard gardener, but is actually Jesus. Both Luke and Mark tell of Jesus in "another form", and Luke also relays a scenario where two disciples walk and talk with the resurrected Jesus for several hours without recognizing it was him. Several Christians in the second century wrote about these things, but you and I have not been allowed to read their gospels, until now.

After studying some of the historical work of Elaine Pagels, Bart D. Ehrman, and John Shelby Spong, one is faced with either continuing to explain the facts of well-researched history away, and the 'gnostic' gospels as "a bunch of Eastern nonsense", or take a long walk along the pier and say to yourself "Oh my gosh!" The Christianity of the latter part of the first century and basically all of the second century, if one was to really do their homework, would better resemble a Deepak Chopra seminar in Sonoma, California than what third and fourth-century Rome has sold us. It is my honest and sincere belief that Jesus himself would feel more at home here (in our century), philosophically, with the Buddhists and new agers.

Very few Christians have any idea that most well renowned Bible scholars now agree that the last *twelve* verses of the gospel of Mark (16:9-20) were actually added much later by an 'unknown to anyone' transcriber. Are these discrepancies not important?

The point being made here is not whether Jesus was crucified, or even that he was revived from a state of medically defined death, but that these are not eyewitness accounts. If the Creator of the universe was directing those ink quills like so many of us were taught He was, would such discrepancies have happened? These are not matters of 'different points of view' (as some like to claim), but flat out different stories of what actually happened. They are in fact contradictions, no matter how much we, or a dozen Christian writers, try to spin them as something else. Many people do not want to talk about this, and many don't even want to know about this. Shouldn't we ask ourselves why?

A Lack of Knowledge

Ask any evangelical Christian if they have any knowledge of how the philosophy of 'orthodoxy' evolved, or for that matter what is the original (second-century) meaning of the "Gnostics," or a "heretic" (the most accurate description of a heretic, by the way, could most certainly be "Jesus"). How many preachers have you heard explaining the differences between the interpretive methods of ancient Jewish Midrash and the more westernized literalist methodology? Most Christians haven't even heard of names like Polycarp, or Marcion, or Irenaeus, or for that matter, even Josephus. Ask any evangelical Christian to give you a short version of how the Latin Vulgate came about and what main issues Jerome faced with that project. What is your knowledge of *Mill's Apparatus*? Did you know that over a period of fifteen hundred years there were not dozens, or hundreds, but (literally) thousands of blatant contradictions, inconsistencies, additions, and deletions throughout the process of formulating what we know today as the "Bible"? In the second and third centuries, Christianity branched out in mainly three different directions: toward Africa, toward the East, and toward Rome. Do you know why Rome won that official contest? Are these the subjects we are supposed to leave in the hands of biased theologians? We don't like politicians telling us 'what's best for us,' but for some odd reason – when it comes to theology, we are much more willing and trusting to take the timid and subservient role as sheeple.

Things We Do *Not* Want to Know About

Did you know that in the gospel of Phillip (an authentic, historically reliable document), Jesus is reported to have been repeatedly kissing Mary Magdalene? The text also shows how this greatly disturbed his disciples, and they questioned Jesus, claiming that he loved her more than them. We, of course, were never allowed to read about this in *our* Bibles, because some people decided that it wasn't an 'inspired' book. Have you ever asked yourself who are the men who were qualified to make those decisions?

The gospel of Thomas, in spite of having striking parallels with the four accepted gospels, sounds more like a Dr. Wayne Dyer P.B.S. Special. It is no surprise why that extremely-valuable gospel was voted out of our Bibles. I have devotionally studied many amazing teachings on the gospel of Thomas, but to most Christians it all sounds like a "bunch of new age nonsense". We completely discount and reject the gnostic gospels mainly because we were told to by theologians we blindly trust. But when we actually take the time and effort to study deeper into second-century history and are willing to listen to the proponents of those early Christians' writings – we shockingly find ourselves learning the deeper things not only about those very spiritual Christians, but also about Jesus himself. We also learn how the Roman church (basically) crushed the beauty of their version of Christianity out of existence, and just how political this power trip to have the 'official' gospel really was. A good place to start is "The Gnostic Gospels" by Elaine Pagels.

What about the missing years of Jesus? There isn't one shred of evidence that Jesus remained in Palestine during those eighteen years. Unknown to most Christians, there are no less than *thirty* different manuscripts and documentation from Turkey to Tibet indicating that Jesus' missing years had him traveling the Old Silk Road through Turkey, Persia, Pakistan, India, Kashmir, and elsewhere. There are also several stories of Jesus having to flee certain areas because of his boldness. Jesus' studying under all the great spiritual (Eastern philosophy) masters of his time is a well-established historical fact in the minds of many throughout these Eastern providences. Jesus is reported to even have foretold the crucifixion that would be awaiting him when he returned to Jerusalem. Even more shocking than this is the amount of evidence that places Jesus back in India after surviving his crucifixion, where he lived to be an old man, and his body is believed to be buried at the Roza Bal Shrine in Kashmir. Did you know that inscribed on the steps of the Takhat Sulaiman (Throne of Solomon Temple) in Kashmir were the words, "At this time Yuz Asaf proclaimed his prophet-hood. Year fifty and four (AD 78). He is Jesus, prophet of the children of Israel"? If we were to be brutally honest with ourselves we would have to admit that it is more than probable that not only the body of Siddhartha Gautama is buried somewhere in Asia on this big, blue planet, but so is the body of Jesus. And the possibility of any living biological life form having ever ascended up into the stratosphere without the aid of an oxygen tank, space suit, or spacecraft, is highly unlikely as well.

Shocking? Why is all this information such a shock to so many Christians? Why do so many vehemently reject such things with no intention whatsoever of taking the time and effort of researching them on their own? If there were even one tenth of this amount of information that kept Jesus in Palestine during his adolescent years, that would be viewed as 'solid and credible evidence', because that would support what we've been told to believe. We truly believe only what we want to believe, don't we? Why is it that any documentation out of the *Middle East* (that supports Christian beliefs) is celebrated and immediately elevated to 'credible' status, but anything (no matter how convincing) out of the *East* is, well, you know, some kind of Indian fable? Is that because we can't trust people from India?

So, the most influential person in all of human history completely disappears for the vast majority of his life (age 2 to 12, age 12 to 29). The good, honest people from the Eastern providences offer us a significant amount of well-documented clues, and we call them "crazy conspiracy theories."

I did not know that there were several prior ancient cultures that claimed their religious leader arrived through a virgin birth? I did not know that John 1:1 ("In the beginning was the Word, and the Word was with God, and the Word was God") is a translated quote from the Hindu Rigveda? The Vedas precede this Bible verse by thousands of years. But why has no pastor spoken of such things? Did you know that the verse that says, "The kingdom of heaven is within you" is a direct quote of an even more ancient verse from an Egyptian proverb? So, do we just brush this all off as 'so much garbage'? Really?

Anyone who has devotionally studied Buddhist writings (dated 550 years before Jesus), can no longer deny that Jesus was not only inspired by these ancient teachings, but actually drew from several of the parables, reformatting them to use in his own ministry.

Someone may say, "Ken! Where are you getting all this nonsense?" And yet, clearly, anyone who even asks such a question shows themselves as one who has not done their own research on these matters. I am only trying to get to the truth. And I am just no longer afraid of what the truth might reveal itself to be. What I have listed here isn't even a drop in the bucket of similar such uncomfortable facts. The reason all of this may sound 'far-fetched' is because the preachers we trusted never brought any of these things to our attention.

Does Fulfilled Prophecy in the Bible Prove Inerrancy?

Where do Bible apologists go next for 'unquestionable' proof that the Bible is God-dictated? They confidently lay the bulk of their 'evidence' on fulfilled prophecies. Who can intelligently argue with that? Well, the answer is science, which is now right on the verge of proving that the past, present, and future are all taking place simultaneously. Crazy? Have you ever wondered what déjà vu is? It is very possible that Old Testament prophets were not shown the future, but simply saw the future (just as some gifted people in modern times have also done), and then began (literally) manifesting and creating the religion they were themselves perpetually creating. Anyone who understands the realities of the Law of Attraction and even a beginner's view of quantum physics also understands how this is more than possible. Albert Einstein once said, "Time is not at all what it seems. It does not flow in only one direction, and the future exists simultaneously with the past." In just recent times, this is actually being proven. Physicist John Wheeler said, "Time is what prevents everything from happening at once." Anyone who wishes to explore these exciting possibilities would do well to obtain a copy of *The Divine Matrix* by Gregg Braden; just one of many resources on this subject.

We're *Always* Arguing From a Premise

So many times when people end up debating a particular set of doctrinal beliefs; they do so with the confident assumption that the main, fundamental things they all agree on are solidly established facts. There are certain things in Christianity called "fundamentals." Although many doctrines are acceptable to question, and even debate, the foundational fundamentals are thought to be beyond questioning.

Here is an example: It is like five people who all agree that hell is a real, physical place doing a five-day authoritatively taught seminar on who goes there, who doesn't, how to avoid it, why it was created, when it was created, what it is like there, whether or not the people who are thrown there get to converse with those in heaven, including an additional class with a teacher who shares his dark and scary NDE story to supposedly give even more 'support' to a doctrine that all five leaders of the seminar agree on. Point being: the entire five-day seminar is based on a *premise* that their (foundational) doctrine of hell is beyond questioning. And we do this same exact thing on a myriad of Bible subjects. When we say the words "gospel," or "salvation," or "forgiveness," or "eternal life," or "heaven" and "hell," or "saved," or "sheep and goats," or "end of the age," or "inspired by God," or "the judgment," or even "born again," we do so with the assumption that all the definitions and interpretations we have been taught about those subjects are correctly formatted, perfectly understood, and beyond questioning.

"But It's in the Bible, Ken!"

In a somewhat heated discussion with a dear Christian friend, she threw her hands up in frustration and said, "Ken! It's in the Bible!" And 'it' probably is, but there are many things in the Bible. Just to mention a few, there's a talking snake; a talking donkey; a crow that delivers food; a man who single handedly kills a thousand fully armed, battle trained soldiers with a bone; a whale that transfers a man across the Mediterranean in the dangerously toxic acids of its stomach; and fifty thousand different animal species from every continent on the planet (including Antarctica) showing up one afternoon somewhere in the Middle East to tamely walk up into a boat that realistically couldn't fit a thousand, let alone a thousand pairs.

Who Said, "God Said"? Who Saw God Do?

We have all heard people say that everything in the Bible is true, but why is it all true? Is it all true because we have proof? Or is it all true because we were told to believe it is? Most people, including myself, would never intelligently question historical events in the Bible that can easily be substantiated by other ancient historians. But what do we do with all the seemingly 'hard to believe' events? Who saw or heard God talking in a loud voice and saying all the things the Bible records Him to have said? The answer? No one. That's who. All those stories were passed down orally, over many generations. And why have all those bigger-than-life, nature defying miracles God supposedly did all throughout the Old Testament come to a screeching halt?

The Tower of Babel

In this well-known passage (Genesis 11: 1-9) God was supposedly not happy with man building a tower that would reach the sky, but apparently has no problem with the International Space Station, or manned missions to Mars. The passage actually states that the reason this needed to be done is because if it wasn't done there would be nothing man wouldn't be able to accomplish. Many literalists will claim that God didn't intervene for the reasons that the text clearly says He did, but because of men's hearts. Like so many other stories in the Old Testament, this appears to be another ancient Jewish bedtime story. Or, the Creator of 500 BILLION other GALAXIES "said" to... whoever was with Him in the sky - "Let us go down there" and confuse their language.

If the Tower of Babel story were actually literal, then God didn't just change the language, but the skeletal structures, color, and facial features. Fortunately, mankind's different languages can be traced to be time-based, area-based evolutions having their origins from other languages. Did God really say, "Let's go down there and stop the humans"? What does your heart tell you? Could it be that the reason there are different languages is the results of thousands of years of the human species migrating to different parts of our planet, and evolving there?

Interestingly, when literalists don't like what a passage clearly says, they do exactly what they accuse the more liberal theologians of... picking and choosing. A good example of this is the Apostle Paul's view of women, and how they should keep their mouths shut in church (1 Corinthians 14: 34-35, 1 Timothy 2: 11-15). The minute these verses are pointed out, they will say, "Oh that was based on a first-century cultural issue." Really? Read it again... The verses are very clear that Paul bases this view of women on the creation story, not first-century culture.

God's Character Painted

Does the Old Testament really show us an accurate character sketch of a God that we should want to emulate? If so, jealousy, anger, and the need for personal revenge are attributes we should also desire. Should we honor the idea of owning a couple of slaves, or condone human sacrifice, mass human genocide, or stoning of our rebellious teens? These are just a few of the traits ancient writers penned about who they thought God was and what He Himself supposedly ordered. For years, scholars have called these the "problem passages."

There are several places in the Bible where God reportedly spoke something that directly goes against the character of Jesus, whom we are told is a mirrored reflection 'of the Father.' What do we do with all those awkward and ugly Old Testament passages that make the Creator of the universe out to be a monster? One ancient writer paints God as benevolent and another describes Him as vengeful and jealous. One writer explains God as "no respecter of persons," but another as an Entity Who has favorites. One writer talks of an always-consistent God, while another speaks of a Creator Who continually changes His mind. We read of a 'God' who in one place tells man, "Thou shalt not kill," and yet in another place He supposedly orders man to commit mass human genocide, including women and children (and taking the spoils, which would fall under 'coveting'). So how do we process that? "Thou shalt not kill, unless I tell you to"? Or perhaps the most popular defense: "God is God and He can kill whomever He wants"? I have even heard people trying to hypothesize the justification of God ordering the killing of children because perhaps He knew that they would one day be a threat to the lineage of Jesus. No, I did not just make that up. But the most popular, and most thoughtless 'defense' of a murderous God is, "Well, God did things differently way back then."

One Old Testament writer records his concepts of an angry Being full of wrath and punishment, and yet another, full of mercy, patience, and forgiveness. And we've been asked (I'm sorry, told) to believe both, and a lot of people have worked very hard and a lot of puzzle pieces have had to be creatively forced together to 'support' that contradictory story. And yet, like they say, the Bible speaks for itself.

Women as property: Deuteronomy 21:10-16

Abortion: Numbers 5:12-22
Slavery: Leviticus 25:44; Exodus 21:20-21
Sex slaves: Exodus 21:7-11
Murder and rape and pillage: Numbers 31:7-18; Zechariah 13:3, 14:1-2; Deuteronomy 13:13-19, 17:2-5, 20:10-14, 22:20-21, 21:18-21, 22:28-29; Hosea 9: 11-16; Leviticus 20:9, 21:9, 24:10-16, 26:21-22; Exodus 12:29-30, 32:27; Ezekiel 9:5-7; Jeremiah 51:20-26; Isaiah 13:15-18; 1 Samuel 15:2-3, and too many more to list.

I am not suggesting that we all throw our Bibles down the hill, but I think it is reasonable to start questioning some of what we believe if we are to maintain any sensible amount of intellectual credibility in the eyes of the world. Don't you?

From What They Thought They Knew

Could it be that ancient writers were simply attempting to explain the unexplainable? Perhaps they experienced exactly what we experience daily with the divine, and tried their best to explain their concepts of those experiences. Even a casual study of ancient history will reveal that they were not the first civilization to forge the concept of an 'up there somewhere' God. For instance, thunder and lightning were seen by the ancient Greeks as God's anger, and rain for the crops was, of course, viewed as God 'providing,' etc. But it wasn't just the weather and earthquakes that had them guessing. What they experienced on a spiritual level was the same never changing, consistently predictable, interactive properties of God's Spiritual Law that you and I experience today. What if this indefinable Law, or Operating System, if you will, literally permeates every single atom throughout the entire universe? You know, the "same yesterday, today, and forever," and "no respecter of persons." Some Old Testament writers used the words "His law is perfect." Other writers talk of God's "faithfulness." One of them reports that "God is not a man that He should lie," suggesting that God is incapable of changing. This almost sounds scientific in nature, does it not?

Unfortunately, some of these ancient writers also added many of their own human concepts and attributes to this unexplainable Source, or 'God.' In no time at all, they had 'Him' ordering things like mass human genocide, stoning people, and even publicly sanctioning the burning of unfaithful women and daughters alive at the stake. Yes, that is in the Bible. Interestingly, there are no such similar ancient Judaic laws for unfaithful men. They indeed created a God in their own image. They used Him to justify their wars, and the most unspeakable human rights atrocities imaginable. Some ancient writers painted God as a human characteristic-like Being that better represents an emotionally wounded, psychologically imbalanced, abusive, alcoholic husband and father who demands respect from his wife and children, or else. Is this 'God' Who suffers from some serious anger management, jealousy, and personal revenge issues, the God of reality, or of religion?

Then How Can We Know What Is True?

I can't tell you how many times my work on this subject has been passionately questioned by those who oppose such questionings. Here are just a few of those actual, word-for-word challenges:

"Ken, where then is your foundation? If you don't believe the entire Bible is true and divinely inspired, then you have no foundation."

"Where do you get your truth from then, and what are you basing it on?"

"How do you determine whether or not a particular text is inspired or not?"

"Ken, when you say the truth was not trapped in one book (the Christian Bible), you might as well just say that you deny Christ himself."

"Yeah Ken, I guess God lacks the ability to reveal Himself to His creatures in written form. Where do you people come from?!"

"If the Bible is not totally inspired by God then you and I have no way of knowing God personally and relationally."

"Ken, life has to have explanations and answers to the whys of life's questions, and the biblical accounts."

"So Ken, if God's authorship of various texts is debatable, how do you decide which parts represent God accurately and which parts don't?"

"If God's Word (the Christian Bible) is fallible with mistakes, contradictions, and inconsistencies, then we have nothing substantial to build our faith upon. To believe that is a life built without a solid foundation, mere sinking sand!"

But wait a minute. Doesn't the Bible say something about God's law being written on man's hearts (Hebrews 10:16), and that we will need no man to teach us because we will know the truth (1 John 2:27)? How is that possible? Have we forgotten about those verses? Is the truth not in us? Why, oh why, are we afraid of such a gift from our Creator? I love the Bible, but is the truth really somehow, exclusively trapped in only that one book? Our indoctrinated heads have a hard time stepping out of that mystically romantic, ancient Middle East and into a place of actually thinking our own (twenty-first century) thoughts and formulating our own interpretations of truths, not only in the Bible but outside of the Bible. And yet, some of the statements I just shared reveal that some would indeed feel quite lost without their Bibles.

Deciphering the Truth at Starbucks

One sincere fellow said this, "If we can't believe everything in the Bible is true, then we can't believe anything in the Bible is true." He also added, "How are we to tell what is true and what isn't? Ken, if you do not believe the Bible, then you have no faith. You've thrown the baby out with the bathwater." But that's like saying, "If we can't believe everything said at our local Starbucks, then we can't believe anything ever said at our local Starbucks." Also, how are we to tell what is true or not at Starbucks? Are we really that helpless? We determine whether or not something is 'true or not' with our hearts. I do not believe that God gave us intuition, logic, and the aptitude for reasoning things out so we could trade them all in for a book. Do you?

Is God 'On the Throne'?

When someone says, "God is still on the throne," do they really believe that a Divine Consciousness that brought about the entire universe sits on an actual chair somewhere in outer space, or that Jesus sits in another chair just to His right? Words like "chair" and "throne" and "kings" and "servants" and "kingdoms" are human things. And so are this list of things… Father/son relationships, livestock tending, books, salvation, wrath, rewards, punishment, guilt, innocence, disciplining those we love, gifts, owing, paying, answering requests, allowing, speaking, caring, granting immunity, acquittal and absolution, faithfulness, disobedience, judgment, mansions, streets, gold, gates, pearls, treasures, things that are "above" or "below," etc. These are all human characteristics, and descriptions of human things and activities, are they not? Since the Jewish culture views The Torah metaphorically, shouldn't the religion that finds its roots in Judaism also consider doing the same?

Is the Bible not full of analogies and metaphors that were intended to convey deeper spiritual realities that we are just now beginning to comprehend? Is God interacting with us, or are we interacting with God? Is our 'personal relationship' with God more accurately a relationship with ourselves as we interact with Spiritual Law? These are all valid and reasonable questions. And yet by asking them, we often get branded as someone who is "trying to discredit the Holy Word of God," and thus supposedly becoming an enemy of both Jesus and the church.

Is there really some sort of Being somewhere in outer space that is 'listening to' or 'answering' our prayers in the same way someone would call their uncle on the phone? Is such a human-like relationship dynamic really taking place? Or is it much bigger than that?

The Rope Swing (and the Creation of Five Religions)

On an old dirt road there is a particular bend next to a scenic pull-off by a beautiful river. A large tree leans majestically over the water with a rope for swinging over the deeper part for a refreshing splash. Autumn leaves frame the entire scene like one of those old covered bridge calendar photos. The water ripples consistently around the bend, bubbling and swirling over a fallen tree as the gentle current moves in a never changing motion.

Five people are invited to visit the spot so they can write a story of their experience.

One person swings out over the deep and plunges into the refreshing cool water. Another person simply sits on a rock and feels the current rushing around their feet. One person brings a fishing pole and catches enough dinner for two families. And yet another person simply opens the door on their car, sits there with a cup of tea, enjoying the inspiring view. The fifth one slips under the surface with goggles and swims underwater, letting the current offer the most amazing show of the beauty below as he moves downstream.

Then, all five of them retire at the cabin to write their stories. When all five stories are read aloud, the five people begin to argue about the different experiences.

The Separation Begins

The first person debates how jumping in the river head first from the rope swing is the only one true way to be able to say that you 'know' and have 'truly experienced' the river and its beauty.

The second person insists that until you respect the river enough, and start by only inserting your feet, you take the river for granted and risk losing your reverential awe for it.

The third person argues that if you do nothing practical with what the river offers in terms of provision, then you are missing the whole point of the river.

The fourth person tells an amazing story of meditation and how he was the only one who noticed the dance of the dragonflies in the sunbeams that filtered down through the leaves, only to sparkle on the river's surface.

The fifth person just shakes his head with an obvious air of arrogance, remembering the amazing contours of the river's bottom and the fish swimming around him.

Conclusions About "The River"

1. The river never changes, nor does it make itself different for anyone, but is the same river today, yesterday, and tomorrow, and even a year from now.

WHAT ABOUT BIBLE INERRANCY?

2. The river doesn't care if you jump, swim, fish, relax, drink, or even just meditate.

3. The river itself doesn't have a different relationship with person #2 than it has with person #5; it is the people who are different, not the river. It doesn't tailor its experience (or relationship) differently for you than it does for anyone else. The river is "no respecter of persons," and it treats no thing and no one differently, for to do so would make it not a river, but a person.

Perhaps the reason our relationship with God is 'personal' is not because there's some Guy in the Sky dispensing blessings on some while withholding blessings from others, protecting some while not protecting others, or granting you gifts, depending on if you've been good or bad or upon what you do or don't deserve. We reap what we sow, and isn't that more about the results of our own thoughts and choices? Are we not ourselves creating, attracting, and manifesting those realities into our own lives with our desires, intentions, imaginations, feelings, thoughts, and yes, even faith? The Law of Attraction? Is that even a possibility?

Six

BIRTH CANAL MEMORIES

In a short sentence: Paradigm shifts are painful. In the church world, it is considered 'normal' to seriously question anything that is not 'Christian.' Also thought of as reasonable is the prospect of people leaving other philosophies and religions to convert to the Christian faith. Being raised as a Christian and then later in life adopting philosophies outside of that realm is not so welcomed, nor easily accepted as having any degree of wisdom or theological credibility. Although you may hear some preachers say that they enthusiastically welcome questions, time and personal experience have shown me that this is only true if the question askers are uneducated, respectfully timid, and unable to debate persuasively.

What's This Whole 'Law of Attraction' Thing About?

The Bible, including the teachings of Jesus, were undoubtedly written and spoken in the language, context, and concepts of the times. Throughout the history of mankind, people have experienced 'The River' (God), and in their explorative enthusiasm of realizing that God has predictable character (or attributes), wrongfully concluded that 'The River' was like them, and that's exactly how they wrote the entire story; thus, assigning their human attributes to their concepts of God. But could it be that a universe-wide Spiritual Law is actually "God"? Could it be that God is actually more like a 'Program' than a 'Person,' much like the operating system on your computer? Is that really such an absurd possibility? Could there be any validity to such a 'new to us,' seemingly impersonal philosophy?

Please consider this. The language we use to get what we want from our computer is a series of clicks, drags, drops, cuts, pastes, and typing of certain particular keys. If this sowing and reaping/Law of Reciprocity/Law of Attraction is true, then the language we are using to get what we need and want from our Source/God/Spiritual Law is feelings, thoughts, intention, imagination, passion, desire, attitudes, emotions, expectations, and faith. "As a man thinketh, so is he." With this philosophy, every single thought is a 'prayer.' Could that actually be true? No?

Imagine for a moment that this Spiritual Law/Program (we call "God") is the same molecular level 'operating system' throughout the entire universe of 500 billion different galaxies. If not, then God would not truly be the same (in all locations) yesterday, today, and forever. Is it even possible that assigning human characteristics to this unexplainable Source was the only way ancient men could somehow explain such an interactive Provision-based Law to the people of their time? It supplied them with everything they could possibly want or need. When they acted selfishly and in a fashion that was opposite of the character or 'properties' of this originating Source, they reaped the harvest of those choices; hence their concepts of continually being either 'rewarded or punished' by an actual, well, personality, or ... Being.

Perhaps these ancient people, having truly experienced this *law* and its Father-like (reward and punishment) properties, at one point 'decided' that *it* is a 'Person,' much like the Zeus in the sky the Greeks had conceptualized, or the heavenly gods of Ra and Amun and Isis of the ancient Egyptians. The writers of the Bible wrote so romantically about this 'God,' as they indeed should have. And we have all benefited greatly from their work, but now we are entering a new age where even more information is being revealed. Yes, it is.

Dancing With God

Could it be that the reason we have a 'personal relationship with God' is not because God is a Person, but because we are? My 'shocking to some' proposal is that God is not interacting with us. We are interacting with an eternally fixed

Law that man has named "God." Wow! I can't believe I just said that! Therefore, we are not experiencing an external Being Who is 'doing things' in our lives. What we are (actually) experiencing is ourselves interacting with that fixed Law, and we are doing it with the language of thoughts, feelings, and faith, literally attracting those results into our own lives. I believe our 'relationship' with God, in truth, is actually more scientific in nature than we are yet even comfortable with entertaining, let alone accepting. My personal belief is that our 'requests' are not being 'granted' or 'approved' because of a (human-like) decision being made by an actual Being somewhere out in the cosmos, but that we are, perhaps unknowingly, 'dancing with God' with every thought we think.

Crazy? Compared to What?

Is there really a Guy in the Sky, Santa Claus-like, human characteristic Entity making (actual) minute-by-minute decisions on who to bless and who not to bless, who to protect and who not to protect, who to answer and who not to answer, who to reward and who to punish, who to enlighten and who to withhold enlightenment from, what to allow and what not to allow? Are these not the Zeus-like human concepts of ancient men? Have we lost the ability to be totally honest about this?

Who is really 'in control' and moving all the pieces? Is it us, or some 'separate from us,' 'out there somewhere' God? What if neither God nor some invisible monster in the forest out behind our house has anything to do with our lives? What if it is all us? What if it has always been us? Are we ready for that level of personal life responsibility? I believe when we finally get to the bottom of these mysteries in the next few decades, the truths on these matters will not make God smaller, but actually bigger. After all, it is the truth that sets us free, even if it is uncomfortable at first.

Uncharted Territory

Uncharted territory makes us very nervous, because we have no control over what we are about to discover, and therefore we lack the authoritative theological confidence to be ready to answer most of the questions people may ask. This is the main reason most people seldom cultivate the unknown: fear and insecurity of not having all the answers. The ironic thing about this is that we don't have all the answers now, but have just been convinced that we do. Again, that's religion in a nutshell: deciding that the old information is all the information. It is not. The main trouble with the more progressive (out-of-the-Christian-box) theology of our time is that if we find out any of it is true, then we have to go back to the drawing board about some of our inherited, treasured doctrines, and we don't want to have to go through that awkward process. Let's just be honest.

My friend, Gaddy Gose, from San Jose, California, says this…

> There comes a point in the search for truth where you have to make a choice. Either you continue on and accept the possibility that everything you've been taught to believe is wrong or you turn back to safety. It takes someone with a really good reason to continue to move past this point - people must be intrinsically driven by something greater than what they have before they let go of everything they know. This leap of faith goes far beyond security - it is absolute vulnerability. It's reaching that last part of the map where nothing beyond is known and moving into that jungle of new frontiers. No landmarks, no paths back to safety, no guarantees - just a trust that somehow, some way, there must be more past this border you've never crossed before.

Some people are just wired to want to know the newly revealed truth discoveries, regardless of the cost. Others would rather default to old, inherited paradigms, because of the cost the newly revealed truth might demand. For so long, civilization has been told to accept that the enchantment of life is in magic passages, sayings, and declarations, God-triggering beliefs, magic people, personages and particular actions that supposedly 'get God's attention,' spurring 'Him' to 'do' something on a person's behalf, all the while not realizing that the most magical ingredient in the entire life process, is us.

Even prayer, in this very generation, is being re-thought and re-considered. But who wants to learn or even contemplate a new, different philosophy on how prayer works? No one. So we will leave that to our grandchildren to figure out, while we hold fast to the old-school mentalities, rather than be challenged with change.

Is God Talking To Us?

Why isn't God still audibly talking to mankind from the clouds or mountaintops like He supposedly did all throughout the Old Testament? I know that some highly esteemed, nineteenth-century Bible commentators would say it is because "now that we have the Holy Spirit to guide us, God chose to stop speaking audibly." That sounds about as convincing as someone's guess on why 'God allows' an earthquake to destroy a children's hospital.

Could it be that hearing from God is in reality us hearing from ourselves? Is there really a 'separate from us' Entity (or Being) out there somewhere who makes a decision one sunny afternoon to talk to us? Shocking as it may be, there are other viable schools of thought about this. Uell S. Anderson, in his timeless classic *Three Magic Words* submits an interesting concept that we are all a part of what he calls the "Divine Mind." Other spiritual writers refer to us being a 'part of God' and largely unaware co-creators with God. One of my most valuable life mentors, Dr. Wayne Dyer, uses the term "spark," proposing that we are a spark of our originating "Source," and therefore intimately connected to that Source. A very close friend of mine named Shirley said this: "We are all God peering out from our own eyes with the simple job of evolution and exploration of this universe from our point of God's consciousness."

Defining the Divine

Every person's experiences with the Divine are very real, and I would never question the reality of them. What is in question for all of us, however, are all the inherited, mostly mythological definitions of those experiences that we have been given by others. The problem lies in religious men at one point stepping up and saying, "Let us authoritatively tell you exactly what you are experiencing." But it didn't stop there. They went on to say, "If anyone tells you differently, they are your enemy." And that is why there are still people walking around who swear that you cannot possibly know, experience, or love God and people correctly without being from their particular faith. Yes, there are actually people who still believe that.

Interestingly, getting your miracle experiences redefined by more progressive theology doesn't stop the miracles. As a matter of (experienced) fact, miracles often become even more commonplace. But how is that even possible? It is possible because reality doesn't stop being reality just because you remove religion from it. Our experiences with the Divine have been explained and defined in a social relationship format. But does that make this 'personal relationship' dynamic a fact? Or is it just how we have been programmed to understand or interpret all the things we experience?

Knowing Jesus

Can we really know Jesus personally and not know him personally at the same time? Many people actually think we can. I know that something within us resonates with the truths Jesus taught. We may be quite aware of how that truth itself has been revealed in our personal lives, but can we actually 'know' this same Jesus who walked around in the Middle East some 2000 years ago on a social, person-to-person basis?

When someone says, "I know Jesus and have a personal relationship with him," I have to revert back to my own observation of forty-plus years in the church. I remember all the people who said they 'knew' Jesus personally and yet also believed he was teaching all sorts of crazy things they now no longer believe. How can we say that we know someone personally and then be totally wrong about some of the most fundamental things that person stands for? Just over the last few decades the words of Jesus have been used to judge people, brand people, separate people, justify banishing people, socially disregarding them as lost, and even seeing them as hell bound.

I am convinced that if we wanted to actually know Jesus we would have to build a time machine that placed us on that dusty, first-century, camel-trodden road next to him. I am guessing that this would also be the case for personally 'knowing' the apostle Paul, Alexander the Great, Christopher Columbus, Abraham Lincoln, or even John F. Kennedy for that matter. If such a time machine existed we may end up standing next to Jesus himself asking where we might find a man named Jesus, because he probably wouldn't fit our 'knowing' of who he was. Sometimes what we think we know and what we actually know are two different things.

I'm going to say it. By making Jesus more than he was, we have actually rendered him less than he was, and in the process of Deifying him for the express purpose of (basically) replacing Moses with Jesus and starting a new (obligation-based) religion, we have completely missed much of the very essence of his teachings. How could this have happened? Why do you suppose many Christian's theology more closely represents the philosophies of the Fox News Network, the Republican Party, and conservative talk radio than the very teachings of Jesus himself? How do you honestly think that happened (because it did, you know)? How on earth did we get such an 'us vs. them' religion from the teachings of Jesus?

Knowing God

When we say we know God, are we not simply saying that we have experienced the character or properties of God's Spiritual Law? Our interactions and 'relationship' between this mysterious 'Source' and ourselves are so predictable and vividly scientific in nature. We know it in our hearts, and I believe we always have known it. Is it possible that we are unknowingly translating that experience into a sort of 'I'm down here and He's up there somewhere,' human-based (social) relationship? Is it not possible that what we think is a Father/Son type of 'personal relationship' is actually more scientific in nature? And if so, does it really matter? I do realize that much of our relationship with God was in fact framed in the Bible as a human-like characteristic 'personal relationship.' But we are talking about a time when even Bible scriptures clearly reveal that the writers thought the sun was orbiting a flat earth. Was Jesus telling us that God is a Father-like Being Who lives somewhere in outer space, or was he not speaking to his first-century audience in the realm of their inherited ancient concepts?

Perhaps the subject at hand is not so much about knowing God or Jesus 'personally,' but becoming more keenly acquainted with ourselves, and with our own intimate, eternal connectedness to our Source. I know this rings true with the hearts of many of my readers. Our very real experiences are not dependent upon the definitions or explanations being correct, but because the science of it all works regardless of how it is defined or understood. It is not inconceivable that one could call God "Bob," having been raised on a deserted island with that teaching, and be absolutely certain of a personal, interactive, communicative relationship with "Bob," or for that matter, the Great White Mother Humpback Whale of Andromeda. The point I am getting at is that in all actuality there may not be a magic Person, magic words, or magic sayings, nor exclusively stringent written procedures and protocols that create the miracles, but simply faith alone, regardless of doctrine or ideology. That, of course, completely does away with an 'us vs. them' religion, and that is what many find much too difficult to relinquish. And like the rich, young ruler, they turn and walk away.

Would the Real Jesus Please Stand Up?

Throughout the New Testament we find Jesus talking about two very separate subjects...

1. An upcoming regional war between Rome and Jerusalem that was only 35 to 37 years away.

2. Basic, very valuable spiritual teachings that are timeless in relevance and application.

The disturbing, and very unfortunate thing is that theologians (completely unaware) mixed and meshed these two very separate things together in such a "seamless" fashion - that all sorts of damage was done, resulting in the creation of some of the most exegetically-schizophrenic religious doctrines of all time. Thankfully, this very generation is working overtime in finally correcting many of the quite damaging things this has caused. We are not nearing the END of finally getting the Bible all figured out, but indeed nearing the very BEGINNING of such things.

Here comes Jesus to Jerusalem, and other than his warnings about a first-century devastating war with the Romans, he starts teaching philosophy that is much closer aligned with Eastern religious teachings than ancient Judaism. In fact, Judaism, if we can be honest with ourselves, was an extremely separatist, exclusive, racist philosophy based upon them seeing themselves as God's favorite humans, and everyone else as low as dogs. Most interactions Jesus had with the Scribes and Pharisees reveal this. Jesus comes on the scene teaching oneness, inclusiveness, actually praying that all men would be just as 'one' with God as he is. Yes, he actually taught that. But we, of course, have been convinced that he was establishing 'the trinity' with those verses.

If we look closely, what we see him doing is presenting a view of God that didn't just differ from his ancestors, but was almost opposite in some cases. Hence, "you have heard that it is written… but I tell you…" He taught of the character of a much different God than the one even the current twenty-first century church teaches about. If one truly thinks all his lessons completely through, one will find that he taught us to surpass even the character of the 'God' that Old Testament writers talked about. If we truly took the time and the thought of looking at many of the principles he taught, we would shockingly discover that he was not the 'Jesus' our parents' theologians had built for us. His teachings were in fact more *Eastern* than *Middle* Eastern. Yes, I just did say that.

I'm going to say something that I never thought I would ever say. I believe we have yet to meet the real Jesus, but that over the next twenty to thirty years, we will discover who he truly was and what he truly taught, and in doing so, we will also discover his main message to be something quite different than what mainstream Christianity has inherited, promoted, and fiercely protected for so long. Truth be told, many 'followers of Jesus' are not following Jesus; they are following a form of 'inherited Christianity.'

'Our' God Reigns, Not Your 'god'

There's a reason the religious and atheist alike cry at the movies, hurt for the hurting, and are shocked by injustice. There's a reason both can be found on the walk for more funding for breast cancer or a local children's hospital, or side-by-side digging through the rubble for survivors after a hurricane. We are truly one, we always have been, and the only separation is the separation in our minds and in our religions. Guess what our hearts have always known?

Many assume, just because their personal experience within a particular religion is so real and wonderful, that anyone outside of that particular faith claiming to also know God or to have experienced God or report that they are truly happy are simply (and unknowingly) referring to an alternative or counterfeit experience to the real experience that can only be had within one particular religion: '*My* religion,' etc. It goes something like this: "Since my experiences in my religion are so vivid and beautiful, all other religions must therefore be either copies or counterfeits."

Do We Still Believe in Santa Claus?

I am not using a Santa Claus analogy as a way of mocking or belittling people's faith in God. It is simply a fitting equivalence of how many still view God and the workings of God. "He sees you when you're sleeping. He knows when you're awake. He knows when you've been bad or good, so be good for goodness sake." This well-known holiday jingle is describing a supernatural human-like being. He flies through the sky in a sleigh, and knows just where to drop which presents. It reminds me of the song I sang in Sunday school as a child: "Be careful little hands what you touch, be careful little eyes what you see, be careful little ears what you hear ... because God is up above and He's looking down in love. So be careful little hands, eyes, ears." Irreverent or not, Santa Claus is the closest description of how many people have been taught to view God, and from a very young age. It is ironic that those who are against teaching their children about the fictitious character called 'Santa' who lives in the North Pole also teach their children that God is pretty much the same fictitious character, but you know, 'for real.' The way in which we were taught to view God actually has more to do with ancient Greece than ancient Judaism.

Building Denominations on Results

The reason every religion and denomination swears their doctrines are the closest to the truth is because they all get results, e.g., 'answered prayer,' spiritual awakening, and even miracles. Is it any wonder why Christianity is the only religion with thousands of different denominations? People from every religion on the planet are experiencing the awakening and spiritual enlightenment many have experienced within the framework of Christianity. Although this is so very clear to some, it is also strongly rejected by others who still sincerely believe that only their particular religion can produce such life-altering realities.

All Those Other Religions

Recently a man told me, "Yeah, I've studied all those other religions and they're all basically counterfeits of Christianity." I then asked him a question that left him a bit confused: "What did you think of the people themselves?" As the conversation went on, I quickly discovered that his "study of all those other religions" took place in a classroom in the basement of his church. He didn't do as I and others have done, making the effort to actually spend time with the people, meet with their clergy, discover those common denominators, see God in their eyes, break bread and spend time in fellowship with them, and listen to their stories. This church basement scenario, in all practicality, would be the equivalence of trying to get to know people from the Democrat Party by going fishing with the leaders of the Republican Party, or vice versa.

Give Me That Ole Time Religion

The reason that 'ole time religion' produces results is the same reason my friend in Montana can do 'energy work' on my neck in Seattle (from her home in Montana) and my neck pain is healed. Just recently, after experiencing a seriously bruised rib, I shared my affliction with my friends on Facebook. A person from a different part of the world, said this, "Ken, envision this....We all send a mental picture of the pure, healing, white light of God to surround the hurt area in your/our body and each of us puts our hand on our bodies which are all ONE and you accept our love and heal supernaturally fast. You might be very surprised friend, in the morning!" The next morning I was completely pain free. How are these outside-the-Christian-box people able to do this? They are interacting with the same exact Source (with different names and definitions). This is actually old news in some circles. When my sister fell on the ice as a teenager, she lost her vision. My mom called the elders of the church just as she had been taught with first-century religious text to do. They anointed her with oil (also according to Bible verses), prayed an agreed prayer of faith, and she was instantly healed. I saw it with my own eyes. Does that mean that this particular methodology is the only way for that to take place? Absolutely not. Was it wonderful and life changing? Of course it was. And you can put it in a box if you would like -- many people do -- but it will not stay in that box.

Something deep within me has always been whispering, "We are missing something here, something so much bigger. There is something more pure and natural, with more freedom that we've overlooked. Life itself just has to be a whole lot less complicated and a whole lot more simple than what we have been taught."

This *Thing*, this *Power*, this *Intelligence*, this *Love*, this '*God*,' this *Nature*, this *Voice* is empowering people all over the world with its wisdom and its knowledge of how the universe really works, and who we really are. And It is doing it all without our permission. Imagine that! What is this Great Spirit, or *Revealer*, as the ancient American Indians once called it? It doesn't care about your race or station in life, what church you go to, what religion or culture you grew up in, if you're rich or poor, simple, genius, straight, or gay. And it doesn't care if you are at this very moment forming negative judgments because I used the word "It" instead of the word "He." It can't be boxed in. It won't be. We are only kidding ourselves to think we have a corner on this market called 'truth,' or 'God,' or 'Source.' It colors way outside of our lines and soars high above our concepts. It is not human, with human characteristics, as so many of us have been taught by the ancient writers.

Is God in Control Here, Or Are We?

God and Truth do not change. What does change, and must change, is our understanding of both. Throughout history, this has been the case, and our generation will be no exception to that rule. For centuries, anytime there is a crisis, whether it is a death in the family or a nation at war, there has always been a local pastor or priest to comfort us and offer some kind of *meaning* or *explanation* in our time of confusion, grief, and sorrow, with those famous words: "God is in control." So, when we get unexpectedly laid off from our job, or our home goes into foreclosure, or the economy plummets, or a plane crashes, the message is the same: "God is in control." But is that really true? I began to ask myself, "Could it be that God has chosen for us to be in control here?" But again, do we really want that level of personal responsibility? If we can either credit God or blame the devil, then that will keep us monk-like and undeserving as benefactors, or excuse us for living the life of a victim. That kills two birds with one stone. It ensures that we are guarded from being arrogant in thinking we are in control of our own life's outcomes, and also guards us from having to be completely responsible for our own lack of personal growth.

Allow, or Not to Allow. Protect, or Not to Protect.

The weather and the planet do what they do. The geological rumblings of our planet's tectonic plates shift and move as 'set in motion,' natural elements, which naturally create things like tsunamis, earthquakes, and volcanoes. Is it possible, that our Source controls only two things: the maintenance of the atom, and the consistency of Spiritual Law? Is that even possible? Do we still believe that God somehow 'allows' certain people to die in natural disasters while 'not allowing' others to die, protecting some while basically ignoring the desperate cries of others? How many subjects like this are we supposed to keep lazily applying that same old answer to: "There are just some things we will never know"?

Does God Care, or *Is* God Care?

How is it that God cares about my dental appointment going well, or whether or not it rains on my granddaughter's outdoor wedding, but not care about a forty-foot wall of water approaching the coast of Japan? Does God care enough to delay me from getting on the freeway to avoid a multiple vehicle pileup, while at that exact same time not care about a firing squad gunning down thirty innocent people on the other side of the globe? Is God really helping me locate my car keys or giving some NFL player the athletic advantage in order to make a game-winning touchdown, while at the same time not helping some poor child who is dying of dehydration and malnutrition in some no name Ethiopian village?

Is it possible that it is not so much that God *cares*, but that God *is* care? And is it possible that this human word 'care' is actually a metaphor of something more scientific in nature? I have often wondered how God can *care* about my frustrated social drama with a co-worker and yet during that same hour not be all that concerned about a man suiting up in full combat gear with extra ammo outside of a local movie theater in Colorado? God 'cares' whether or not your high school kid graduates, but not enough to stop some criminally ill man from dragging a grade school girl back into the forest? Are we missing something here? Because if I, a mere human being, witnessed such a horrific thing, and had the power to stop it, I certainly would. Does reality and nature show a different picture than what we have been told by preachers? I think the answer is obvious.

Does God 'Feed the Birds'?

When Jesus said the Father feeds the birds (Matthew 6:25/26), was he saying that God makes sure every year that the robins have enough worms or that the sparrows have a good supply of bugs? If that were the case, then there wouldn't be any children starving in Ethiopia. Wasn't this more of a scientific statement about a provision principle he wanted them to understand? Certainly God would not (literally) 'feed the birds' but not the starving children. And yet looking at reality, it would certainly appear that way if we were to take that verse literally. If we are going to start taking all Bible verses literally, where do we draw the line? There is so much ancient Middle Eastern (and Eastern) poetry and poetic expressionistic wording weaved all throughout both the Old and New Testament culture of Israel. If this isn't vividly clear to us by now, then we are more desirous of religion-based alternatives to reality than we had thought.

Is God 'Doing a New Thing,' Or Are We Simply Accessing a Very Old Thing?

What if what we thought was God 'doing' things was actually *us* doing things with our interactive language of thoughts, feelings, and expectations? What if the only thing God 'does' was done a hundred billion years ago in a one-time-only act of creation, and now we are simply accessing that provision with the Law of Attraction? Is that even possible?

When we interact properly with that Spiritual Law (whether consciously or not) 'miracles' often happen. Our first thought, of course, is that somehow our Guy in the Sky 'God' looked down from somewhere above us (or around us) and made a conscious decision to 'do' an action. But what if it was actually *us*, and an action that *we* took, interacting with a fixed Spiritual Law? With this view everything that happens to us today has nothing to do with what a 'separate from us' God is doing, nor what some evil, invisible monster is doing. This is not new thinking. People have been pondering ideas like these throughout the ages. We have been taught that there is the natural world, and then there is the spiritual world. It is also not a *new thought* that perhaps they are one and the same? This very generation is just now beginning to scratch the surface on these things, but oh, what a beautiful surface!

What if the magic part of life is *us*? What if the *real* reason you went to the grocery store where you ran into Sharon is because you needed milk and bread? And maybe the reason you ran into Sharon is either because she just happened to be at the same store at the same time, or because you are somehow intimately connected to her socially, emotionally, or on some deeper level that we have yet to discover. I submit that separating ourselves from this magnificent process is actually belittling of who and what we truly are. Removing ourselves from the magic of life as if we are nothing more than God's otherwise worthless little puppets, is not 'being humble,' it is basically saying, "I don't deserve to be amazing."

I love what Marianne Williamson said:

> Our deepest fear is not that we are inadequate. Our deepest fear is that we are powerful beyond measure. It is our light, not our darkness that most frightens us. We ask ourselves, "Who am I to be brilliant, gorgeous, talented, fabulous?" Actually, who are you *not* to be? You are a child of God. Your playing small does not serve the world. There is nothing enlightened about shrinking so that other people won't feel insecure around you. We are all meant to shine, as children do. We were born to make manifest the glory of God that is within us. It's not just in some of us; it's in everyone. And as we let our own light shine, we unconsciously give other people permission to do the same. As we are liberated from our own fear, our presence automatically liberates others.

The Six-Week Spiritual Law Test

Everyone on the planet has experienced the scientific consistency and predictability of God's 'operating system' of Spiritual Law. The following is a test that none of us need to take, because we have all experienced the results of this test already.

For six weeks: live your life negatively, angry, selfish, pessimistic, grumbling, complaining, worrying, being impatient and upset about the traffic, etc., and witness how almost all of the magic in your life comes to a screeching halt in your relationships, in your business, in your creativity, in your entire life, and if you continue with this lifestyle you will eventually watch the actual destruction and death of many things valuable in your life.

Then, for six weeks: live your life positively, optimistically, giving, speaking words and thoughts of gratitude, encouraging others, thinking of possibilities, giving concerted patience with the traffic, etc., and witness all the magic returning back into your relationships, in your business, in your creativity, in your entire life, and if you continue with this lifestyle, you will eventually watch the actual rebuilding and flowering and blossoming of many things valuable in your life.

We all have experienced this. For some in little ways, for some in huge ways, but for all of us it is undeniable. The main thing about this reality is that it matters not what culture or religion or station in life you are from, because this 'no respecter of persons' Divine Law is actually scientific in nature.

The Science Lesson

When I finally grasped the physical geography and size of our known universe, the days of obligation-based religion were numbered for me.

Three Questions, prefaced by seven amazing considerations:

1. Our planet (with orbiting moon) is traveling through space on a 365-day orbit of our star named Sol at 67,062 miles per hour. The bullet from a rifle only travels around 2,700 miles-per-hour.

2. It is now estimated that our very 'small' (100 thousand light years wide) galaxy contains anywhere from 200 to 300 billion stars, and as many as 100 billion solar systems much like our own.

3. Our galaxy is only one of 500 billion other galaxies. Please stop for a second and really think through those numbers and the physical reality of what is out there, or should I say, around us. So, 500 billion galaxies multiplied by 100 billion solar systems each = WOW!

4. Our particular galaxy is actually quite dull and even colorless compared to many of the *closer* galaxies we have photographed, which far out-glory the appearance of ours in magnificence and beauty.

5. I personally create to my fullest ability wherever I go, whether that is in Minneapolis, Paris, Moscow, or on the surface of the moon. I have a funny feeling that if the Creator of 500 billion galaxies didn't do the same, that would make me more creative than God.

6. It is now an observable, un-debatable fact that our planet is not the beginning of the universe. Our solar system is not anywhere near the center of our own galaxy, nor is our galaxy at the center of the known universe.

7. I sincerely believe that 'God' (whatever 'God' is) is the same "yesterday, today, and forever," always consistent, never changing, 'no respecter of persons,' and as predictable (faithful) as science itself. I actually believe that every single atom throughout the entire universe is permeated with God's 'operating system,' and actually is that system Itself. In religious circles, this is called Spiritual Law - which governs the interactions and responses to every single thought, attitude, choice, and belief. And if that's true, then it is scientifically impossible for 'God' to change or be inconsistent.

The Three Questions

A. Is this 'never changing Law' indeed the same for every single atom in all 500 billion galaxies and in each of their 100 billion solar systems? Or is God unchanging in only this one particular galaxy and in only this one particular solar system where we happen to be living?

B. Do you believe it is logical for a Creator who created us (we create everywhere we go) to fill our particular galaxy with 100 billion other solar systems with absolutely no intelligent life? Please remember, that's only one galaxy. There are 500 billion other galaxies (with 100 billion solar systems each) to ask this same question of.

C. We must understand that this little planet is not God's back yard. If there were millions of billions of other worlds out there with intelligent life on them (a logical supposition), wouldn't they all have the same consistently exact spiritual system that we do here? If so, what sort of uncomfortable ramifications would that have on our religious doctrines? Does God (really) have a favorite religion?

Believe it or not, many Christians don't want there to be other intelligent life forms out there. Most of them don't even want to think about it, and for understandable theological reasons. All of the doctrines of Christianity would not apply to those other millions of billions of worlds, and that changes God and the doctrines of the church into either analogies and metaphors, or worse yet, the manufactured concepts of man. If they concede to the possibility of other worlds with intelligent life, they cannot have Jesus dying multiple millions of billions of times, and that is what keeps them *uninterested* in such things as we are freely and fearlessly discussing here. These largely scientific-based thoughts greatly disturb and challenge the very fundamental fabric of our planet's religions. But if we can be honest, these musings are both logical and reasonable, as are their deductions, the main deduction being: God has no religion. Men have religions. God has galaxies.

When we try to fit all of this scientific information into our ancient inherited religion it does not fit. The most popular defense for this is simply not to think about it, reducing it all to no more than a 'bunch of pretty, sparkly things in the night sky.' Truth be told, many would probably like it all to stay that way.

Let's not forget about "hell"... So, in a universe of 500 billion galaxies, in ONE of those 500 billion galaxies (that only contains 100 billion solar systems) – there is supposedly a place of eternal punishment (which was originally 'created for' an evil, Lex Luthor-like mythological being and his 'angels') for the life forms in one of that particular galaxy's 100 billion solar systems - who refused to follow the rules and 'love God' in accordance with ancient Middle Eastern written procedures and protocols. Now you see the hell doctrine in its proper context.

Microscopic Creature Conversation

Now please imagine two microscopic creatures on *one* grain of sand on our planet 'deciding' that since their holy book does not mention life on any of the other grains of sand on the entire globe, then such a thing is 'probably not true.' That is the same mathematical equivalence of us looking up at the evening sky and saying the same thing of God's universe.

Too Beautiful to Comprehend

I submit that the reason we find it so difficult to even imagine there being millions of billions of other worlds out there with intelligent life like us, is because of our own beauty. We look at the things we have built -- everything from forming a coffee cup out of clay, to the magnificent intricacies of a jet airliner -- and it is so amazing to us that our minds simply cannot comprehend other completely unrelated worlds to have been able to evolve to the point of accomplishing the same or more. And yet, if we were to actually stop and consider the sheer size and scope of the known universe, in light of an incomprehensibly creative Creator, the mathematical probabilities in and of themselves yield nothing short of an almost certainty of our planet's beauties of life being duplicated and multiplied millions of billions of times throughout the cosmos. If not, the known universe that I've described would sure seem like a lot of wasted, meaningless, and purposeless space. Would it not?

A Wonderful Creation Theory

No one knows what, where, or even why God is, but here's a theory, that to me, sounds closer to reality than some of the versions I was taught.

Hundreds of billions of years ago a 'Divine Consciousness' decided to multiply, divide, fractalize, and duplicate Itself, turning Its 'Consciousness' into matter and form, and then purposefully, meaningfully, and intentionally expanded Itself/Himself/Herself, Its Own design and essence and very energy pattern outward, thus selflessly sharing (in the character, creativity, beauty, and love that It is) Its Own 'eternal' DNA in an outward *blast*, or 'Big Bang,' if you will.

Why? Who knows? Perhaps for no other reason than to *share* Itself and thus experience Itself through everyone and everything that was created by this 'expansion,' and to, perhaps, fully experience Itself and express itself through a creative expansion of life, throughout a continually growing universe. Hence, everything is 'connected to God' mainly because on some incomprehensible level, everything is God. Therefore, everything in existence also has the potential of 'knowing God' (Itself) -- becoming consciously acquainted with this originating Source (Itself) in and through the many life forms and creations It has brought about through this evolutionary process.

We really don't know, and even this colorful, perhaps entertaining theory is far from actual reality. Does this all sound crazy, and perhaps farfetched? Again, compared to what? The alternative, as we all know, is a Merlin-type invisible Disney character Who sprinkled pretty, sparkly stars across the night sky with the wave of His hand.

Orbital Mechanics Theory

Just recently a man painted a word picture for me of how "God makes sure that our planet stays in perfect alignment with the sun." I found his story both noble and romantic, and decided to share my personal theory about this.

What if the reason our planet maintains such a precise orbit of our star is because 'it knows' that this is exactly where it needs to be in order to provide the most optimum environment possible for all of its inhabitants? This theory would of course have to be supported by every living system here possessing consciousness and being in continual communication with all others, including the sun itself. In short, our entire solar system is 'alive,' as is our galaxy, and the entire universe. It all has 'consciousness,' therefore 'intelligence' on some 'yet to be understood' level.

Impersonal God?

Someone recently told me that a more scientific approach to God is cold and lacks 'personal relationship.' But when one begins to realize that the 'personal' ingredient is us, this puts the ball in our court rather than in the courtroom of a Zeus-like God that we have all been taught about. Let's ask the million-dollar question: If an always conscious Creator literally weaved Itself into every single atom throughout the entire universe, designed to provide everything all creatures throughout the universe would ever want or need, would we call that 'impersonal'? I think not.

We have been taught to need an 'outside of ourselves,' 'out there somewhere' God who looks down, hears, listens, sees, cares, and loves us, you know, in a similar way one human would for another human. But is this particular model empowering or does it not foster an unhealthy level of dependency? Is this belief system accurate to reality, or indeed the end results of a long string of human concepts pieced together that form a religion with a more manageable God? Neil Donald Walsch calls this Separation Theology, wherein something or someone 'out there' needs to come and help me 'down here.' Could the more progressive theological concepts of today be closer to reality than what the church has taught for years? Could science (natural law) and religion (spiritual law) be inseparable parts of the same exact mystery?

Try, just for a moment to see all ancient religious sagas as unfolding manifestations, indeed evolving creations of those concepts and explanations. What if, by using the interactive language of emotion and thought, ancient man not only wrote their own religions, but also then, with the power they (we) possess, through the Law of Attraction, began to (actually) manifest their futures to coincide with their concepts? Perhaps the greatest shock we evangelical background folks will face is not that there is no 'hell,' nor that Jesus is not coming back, but that there is no 'Santa Claus' type of 'God.'

A Priest in the White House?

Imagine just for a minute the White House being governed by priests and prophets, and American history (via the news stations) being written and broadcasted by

Scribes and Pharisees. Such a bizarre scenario gives us an idea of how a great deal of the Bible was constructed. Imagine our war in Bagdad, or Desert Storm, or Vietnam being written as events that God orchestrated... It would sound something like this... "And God said to His faithful prophet... tell the captains of their aircraft carriers to turn into the wind and travel toward the Suez Canal, for I shall be with you in battle..." Now imagine 3,000 years from now a preacher in some other culture on the other side of the planet standing in a pulpit reading this as though it were a fact.

Question: Is it even a possibility that much of that ancient Middle Eastern text is the result of some religious sect's interpretation of regular wars and natural events? We certainly don't want that to be true, do we? Did God "put" a rainbow in the sky? If so, how is it that I can also "put" a rainbow in the sky by using a simple garden hose and the afternoon sun? Did God use America to bring "judgment" upon twenty-first century Baghdad, or did the men in political power just decide to go to war? News people and political analysts had "foretold" such a thing could happen years before it actually took place. Likewise, could almost any first-century Middle Eastern goat farmer tell you that Rome would probably eventually no longer tolerate the more antagonist Jewish zealots? Or was that a really big surprise when they saw legions of Roman soldiers marching toward Jerusalem in 66 AD? I think these are valid, reasonable questions. Don't you?

Aesop's Fable of the Crow

Religion most certainly has had its place in human history, but maybe we have been looking at them all with the wrong (literal) approach. Remember the old Aesop's fable about the crow that dropped pebbles in the bottle until the water level rose so he could drink the water and live? The moral of the story, of course, was that "You get out of life what you put into it." Imagine if we thought the message of that story was that when crows get thirsty in the desert, they drop pebbles in bottles. Is this not similar to what we have done with those ancient stories in the Bible?

We interpret what we experience within the template of what we have been taught to believe we are experiencing. I have a funny feeling that it is not God who has complicated God.

Natural or Supernatural?

If you don't like the completely freeing, guiltless simplicity of nature, religion will provide you with all sorts of extremely interesting alternatives. And you won't be alone, because many people actually prefer it to reality itself.

Nature and its naked honesty is what we are afraid of most. Nature is the one thing that does not lie. It is consistent, predictable, reasonable, logical, and most of all, verifiable. It is short on fables and fantasies, and big on reality and reason. It doesn't use flying ponies, golden cities in the sky, nor courtrooms in space that await us when we die. It is what it is, and it doesn't change according to our inherited religious beliefs. Nature provides the soft sound of evening crickets as the moon rises over the water. In the morning when we open our door, there is no burning bush or pillar of fire in the sky, just the gentle sound of birds chirping and two joggers talking as they run by. Is the splendor of life itself such a boring alternative to accept as the reality that has always been, or do we need to believe in huge, nature defying, mythological events?

Nature is no respecter of persons -- the same yesterday, today, and forever — throughout the entire universe. It is not spooky and weird and fairytale-like. It makes sense, and is right out in the open, in the light, being shown for exactly what it is, and how it works.

Nature doesn't hide its deeper meanings between the lines in some ancient paragraph. It doesn't change to accommodate our spooky afterlife doctrines. It doesn't pick and choose our neighbors like we want it to, and it doesn't pay any attention to our prejudices. Mankind decided to write a story about God long before they (actually) understood God. And unfortunately, it stuck. I think that is the bottom line, and the main source of man's confusion about God and himself.

No More Flying Chariots

Again, have you ever wondered why all of the huge nature-defying, bigger-than-life miracles all took place either in the distant, unverifiable past or are supposedly yet to happen in the distant, unverifiable future? Have you ever stopped and really thought about that? And all the centuries in between that distant past and distant future – um, well, the sound of a neighbor's dog barking and cars on the freeway. Do I believe in the miraculous and unexplainable? Yes, I do, but there is not one report of an automobile flying like a chariot up to heaven because someone was spiritual enough to skip the dying process, nor food (manna) falling from the sky in modern-day Ethiopia, where they could really use such an event.

It has always struck me as *unusual* how God supposedly created the reality of natural law with its predictable characteristics and limitations, but then also created a religion that makes (His) nature out to be somehow less than enough. I also find it very curious how none of the New Age or New Thought authors present a philosophy that sharply conflicts with reality or somehow negatively paints nature as 'fallen' or the 'second best thing' that we have to, well, settle for as long as we are here in this 'wicked world below.' That should make sense to Creationists who believe that God designed nature and the natural processes of nature. The Bible itself records that God Himself said, "It was good" and that it was also "established forever." So is nature the enemy, or is it the truth? You know, "The way things really are here, and the way things really work here."

Regular People, Regular Ducks

What if the supernatural and the natural are one and the same thing? Is that so hard to imagine? I look out my window and see a regular sunset, the evening chirping of crickets, normal everyday rain with an occasional mudslide, earthquake, tornado, and hurricane. I see regular winter, spring, summer, and fall; regular cars and regular trucks, regular people, and regular ducks. Maybe I'm out on a limb here, but I'm guessing that nature has pretty much always been just as you see it when you're sitting on your front steps. I am quite confident that taking a recording device in a time machine back to 4000 years ago in the Middle East is probably not going to produce an audio recording of God speaking "in a loud voice." My dog isn't going to start talking to me in English because I wasn't willing to listen to 'the people God sent,' and if I am going to Africa on a missions trip and fall off that cruise ship a hundred miles out, no whale is going to give me a ride to Africa because 'God wants me in Africa.'

Many people have been so romanced by those ancient stories, and have been led to believe that more stories just like them are coming sometime in our future. Because of this misinformation, they have actually developed a sort of *irreverence* for nature, and some even borderline on a dissatisfaction of it. Unfortunately, religious teachers have convinced them that life in the here and now is somehow *flawed*, and a part of some 'fallen state,' wherein they view things like growing old and even dying as 'out of God's original plan.' They have also been assured that natural things like aging and death will someday, somehow, be reversed or magically repaired.

Why Do We Have to Die?

A dear Christian woman recently asked me this question: "Why do we have to die?" Please stop for a minute and really think about that question. My answer was simple: Everyone has to die. It is a part of nature, and always has been. Our body will die for the same reason a raccoon or a deer eventually dies. The reason it bothers us is because some well-meaning religious men have told us that there is possibly some way around it. It has been a huge disservice to mankind for theologians to wrongfully teach that some of us may not have to endure that natural transition! They have (literally) convinced people that death of the body is somehow because of some 'original sin' that an ancient human committed that affected the rest of humanity for all time. This is not true, and never has been true. Between that belief and the hell doctrine, the psychological damage has been done, which causes innocent people to fear the afterlife and the dying process. Our bodies eventually dying are as much a part of nature as the leaves turning red, orange, and brown in the fall. Again, it is the truth that sets us free, not hopeful alternatives to the truth.

The 'Hidden Message' in Christian Music

For a project of my own, I listened to a Seattle-based contemporary Christian radio station for only two daily commutes. The main themes in most of the music I heard was about:

1. How terribly hard, almost unbearable, it is 'down here below' in this burdensome world, and;

2. An almost begging, ultra-dependent neediness and crying to 'God up above' to please 'come down' and help us through our day, week, month, year, and life. To me, this seems so contradictory to what many Christians often boldly declare about "Christ in us" and Immanuel (God with us) and "Lo, I am always with you" and "We are the salt of the earth and the light of the world."

3. An emotion-based romance, almost lamenting for some future utopian, off-planet paradise that will be so much better than the life we have to struggle through here in the here and now.

The clear, underlying message in the music revealed a completely different people whose God is very much still 'up there,' separate from them, and they of course, 'down here below.'

Here are just a few statements from the songs I quickly jotted down as I was driving:

- Come down, Oh Lord…
- Shine down on us…
- I'm trusting that God knows what He's doing in my life…
- I can't do this on my own…
- Here I am at the door, praying that You'll let me back in…
- I can focus on the score, but I can never win…
- I'm not strong enough to be what I'm supposed to be…
- This world has nothing for me, this life is not my own…
- I can't trust myself to do what's right…
- I am stained with dirt, prone to gravity…
- Help me find Your will…
- My soul is crushed from the weight of this world…
- Let me know the struggle ends…
- I'm all alone, with the night closing in on me…

- Throw me a lifeline and rescue me...
- God, I need You now...
- When I feel like giving up...
- Without You I fall apart...
- Lord, pull me out of this mess I'm in…
- Lord I know that I've let You down...
- My heart is heavy from what it takes to keep on breathing...
- I was sure by now that You would have reached down...
- When my strength is gone, and I can't carry on...
- When I'm in the storm, under the weight of the world...
- Let me see through Your eyes...
- Oh Lord, I can't hardly breathe without You…
- Please help me to please You more…
- God, please be near…

Here's the irony in all of this; The fifties crowd in the church have abandoned the old hymns, claiming (rightfully) that they were full of incorrect and often depressing doctrines of an earlier generation. Yet this 'contemporary' music is doing the same exact thing, perpetually crying out in helpless desperation to an Entity that is still viewed as being very much separate from us. This continual barrage of sad, desperate dependency actually fosters an emotional, soap opera-like, daily lifestyle. Why would I want that? And so, "Whatsoever things are … think on these things" becomes "Oh, God, please help us make it through the week!" Meanwhile the 'non-Christian' gang is 'making it through the week' just fine.

The radio station's 'top of the hour' jingle statement? "Hope and Encouragement in these Troubled Times." But wait a minute: I'm not troubled. Am I supposed to be troubled? One woman called in and made a statement of which the radio station (actually) saved as something to use repeatedly for their advertisement promo. Here it is, and I quote: "If I am not listening to your radio station at work, I don't have peace." I sincerely wish I were making this stuff up.

I began to realize that it is not the lyrics of these songs that are 'all wrong,' it is the theology. It is the theology that is creating this perpetual ultra-dependency that never progresses beyond a certain point. I have a funny feeling that many of my readers can relate to my conclusions. Even though some of the music styles try to emulate the newer, secular music sounds, it stays seemingly imprisoned within the pop, 'bubble gum' status that still evokes toe tapping from even the oldest pastor. It is just 'progressive' enough to make the Christian music buyer feel that their music is indeed 'contemporary.' Completely unknown to most Christian music lovers, those outside the church see most of it as a religious-driven alternative to quality music.

The Strange Romance for Anywhere Else (But Here)

In some of the songs, there seemed to be a continual psychological love affair for some distant place that is "Oh, so much better than Earth," which sadly creates a strange sort of contempt for the natural world of the here and now. This *boredom* and irreverence for the world we were placed in is strange at best. It is almost as if they wish death would come faster so they could get out of this nasty, horrible place God supposedly called 'good.' One day when God "calls our name" we will "rise on eagle's wings" and finally get to where we really want to be, because "this world is not our home," etc. And can someone please explain to me the romantically euphoric anticipation of one day physically seeing Jesus face-to-face? What on earth is that about? One of the songs I heard was an anthem of wanting to finally be away from this cruel world and be in heaven entitled, "I Can Only Imagine."

Why not imagine the amazing connectedness we already have with both God and our fellow man, right here, right now? Why not imagine a great picnic day at the beach with family, good friends, good food, and fellowship? Why not imagine how you are going to change the world and heal the world and make a difference on a practical level? Why not imagine growing into adulthood, where people eventually grow out of their religiously inherited, soap opera-like, emotional illnesses, becoming all they were meant to become here? Why not stop trying to be a 'good Christian' (as if you owe that to someone), and just focus on becoming a mentally and intellectually and philosophically stable and healthy, professional human being?

Another song that stuck in my mind as odd was of a congregation chanting the words: "Take this world and give me Jesus. This is not where I belong." Excuse me? The planet you were born on is not where you belong? First of all, when people die here, it is not because 'God called their name,' it is because they died. Secondly, why would we want to leave the place where God supposedly placed us? Just recently I watched a preacher pray (and I quote) "Jesus, I'm a stranger in this world, and I don't belong here. You will soon be coming to take me home to where I really belong." The very core of my heart tells me that there is something disturbingly wrong about this philosophy. Especially when you and I both know that this preacher will die of old age just like the rest of us will, as will our children, their children, and their children. A physical location somewhere in outer space called "heaven" is not our home. Earth is our home. Right here, right now.

When I was a child, I remember a small congregation of forty people, an elderly lady playing an old, out-of-tune upright piano, and the pastor waving his hand in cadence with the song "He's coming soon" ("He's coming soon, He's coming soon; With joy we welcome His returning; It may be morn, it may be night or noon—We know He's coming soon.") Another memorable hymn was "The King is Coming" ("The King is coming, the King is coming. I just heard the trumpet sounding and soon His face I'll see. The King is coming, the King is coming. Praise God, He's coming for me.") That was fifty years ago, but now, the church has a host of new songs that they project on a whitewashed wall about how "These are the days of Elijah", and "Living He loved me", and "When the Stars Burn Down", and "We will dance", and "We Shall Behold Him", etc. The list of contemporary songs that romance a soon-coming Jesus are literally too long to list. When 'worshiping' an up-there-somewhere God became 'worshiping worship', I left the building. Just recently an older Christian lady referred to most Pentecostal worship services as the "7-11 song service"; seven songs sung eleven times. To me it becomes not much different than laying flowers and fresh fruit at the base of a statue in some other religion. In reality, it is the same thing with extra emotional romance added.

My friend Mike wrote this:

> Whenever I chanced upon contemporary Christian music, I noticed a common message between the songs: "I am nothing without God. I'm not complete without God. I can't love people without God. I can't do

anything right with my own motives and thoughts." I thought to myself, "Husbands can't be 'gaga' about their wives without Jesus? Mothers can't love their children unconditionally apart from Christianity's beliefs in Jesus? Fathers can't be good fathers outside of Christianity?"

Being that I was raised in a Christian home and church, I was told that everyone who isn't a Christian isn't happy. Sure they might find temporary pleasure in their filthy sins and ungodly activities, but no one has real happiness or peace outside of Christianity. And I believed it because it was force-fed to me my entire life. Then I met my friends, Dave and Sue. They don't go to church, they don't pray to Jesus, and they're two of the happiest and at-peace people I know. They've found happiness in loving themselves, one another, and others. And that's basically the message Jesus came to deliver. But Dave and Sue found that out all on their own and didn't have to buy a pre-packaged version of someone else's beliefs on life and love. Sue reads books from several veins of beliefs and gleans from all of them. I'm starting to do the same. Be free and live life!

Why Young People Are Leaving the Church

Over the last twenty-five years, the young people have been leaving the church at a more alarming rate than the dying off of the honeybees. Not only are they leaving, but they're not going back. Church leadership, in a more than obvious blind quandary about this mass exodus, have repeatedly gathered together in church conference rooms all across America, trying to figure it all out and come up with some practical solutions. As usual, most of them are blaming anything but themselves. Typically, they point judgmentally outward at the public school system's atheistic view of evolution, or at the evil, dark influences of Hollywood and the music industry. Rather than even contemplating their own non-progressing theology, some sixty-five-year-old in the meeting always makes that predictable statement: "What can we do to attract the young people back into our church?"

They all come to an agreement… a 'rock band' worship service with a $40,000 lighting and sound system, or 'all the pizza you can eat' night, or a Bible study and life discussion on a hill overlooking the city, or Wednesday night at a local coffee house instead of in the secondary sanctuary, or a city-wide treasure hunt that seems more appropriate for 12-year-olds, or even to let them have their 'own service' on Monday night (with properly doctrinalized, adult leadership of course).

But they're still leaving, and they're still not going back. Why? They are not leaving the church because it isn't *fun* enough, or *radical* enough, or *cool* enough, or *real* enough, or *messy* enough. They are leaving because it isn't *their* church; it is their parents' church, and their parents' inherited theology. But more accurately, it is because the level of understanding of their parents' religion isn't growing or evolving into an intellectually respectful, more progressively sophisticated awareness, like the world around them is.

At some denominations' "What are we going to do about losing our youth?" youth conference, here comes the tattooed, bed haired, 32-year-old evangelist, with his 'cutting-edge' message to the church, using terms like "revolution" and "radical shift in thinking," claiming that what is missing is 'cultural relevance,' and how we need to be 'able to relate' to today's culture, etc. Even though he is a really cool-looking dude with his $300 shirt and neon-colored sneakers, he has no intention whatsoever of re-thinking, re-analyzing, or re-questioning the last generation's exclusionary, cult-like, separatist interpretations of the scriptures. And guess what, cool-looking dude? It's the separatist, us-and-them theology, not the communicative approach. It is not a matter of smart innovation of a more entertaining church service, or a better performance by the worship team.

The church leadership changes the language and the terminology, but it is still the same theology. And that same old, fifteenth-century view of the universe is continually preached, you know, God still looks down from somewhere just beyond the noon-day clouds, (like the producer in the Truman show) and the devil still creeps around in the dark forest out behind the house (so to speak). God blesses them whenever He personally observes them doing the right thing, and the devil is continually trying to steal their joy, especially when he sees them doing the wrong things.

Young People Leaving the Church (Separate Yourselves)

They have been trained for years to look at the people outside of the church as either sadly lost, deceptive, or even dangerous. And when a young person reports that they've spent some time talking to their Buddhist co-worker about love, they are sharply warned of the dangers of exposing themselves to other philosophies that differ from Christianity.

One churchgoing person recently suggested to me that over the exit sign at the back door of the church there should be a sign that reads, "You are now entering the mission field," not even realizing just how spiritually arrogant that sounds. But the young people aren't swallowing that same separation theology as their parents did. You know the mindset: "We who are in the church are the ones who have the light and love, and the people 'out there' are the ones without the 'real' light and without the 'real' love. So, we who have the love need to go 'out to those' who don't have the love, and we need to 'love' them." And you know, invite them to our 'funner than all the other churches' church, where we can prove to them that we (and our view of Jesus) are what they've been missing their whole life. Problem is, the young, college-aged people don't want a *fun* church any more than a fifty-year-old wants to play laser tag with his co-workers after a management meeting rather than going home to relax with their family.

Young People Leaving the Church (The Demonization of Outsiders)

The younger generation is sees how the church likes to showcase any failed non-Christian life, while at the same time being hush-hush about the divorce rate within the church. They've been assured by the pastor that their non-Christian friends' lives will end up in shambles. Two days earlier that same pastor was doing (unqualified) marriage counseling with a Christian couple whose lives and marriage is in absolute shambles due to a lack of personal maturity, addictions, bitterness, unforgiveness, and past festering, incorrectly-processed childhood wounds (not to mention the extra religious, doctrine-based guilt and low-self-esteem that goes along with it all). Guess who knows what I'm talking about? Every pastor in town. They know that R.E.M.'s "Happy Shiny People Holding Hands" song is not a true depiction of Christians compared to non-Christians.

Young people see non-Christian co-workers who are happy, full of joy and excitement for life, and wonder how that's possible when they've been told it is not. They see friends who swear like sailors who have more fruits of God's Spirit than many Christians they know, and they've observed people from outside of their faith displaying spiritual insight that even their own church leaders lack. There's a level of genuine freedom missing in the lives of their Christian peers, of which many of their non-Christian friends are not lacking. And they've begun to question the older generation defining their non-Christian friends' freedom as rebellion, disobedience, and selfishness.

They've actually taken the time and the effort to read those *scary* and *dangerous* New Age and New Thought-authored books -- you know, the ones their parents and pastors told them not to read. They shockingly discovered that they are not in contradiction to the Bible at all, but simply a different, and often more reasonable interpretation of both God and the teachings of Jesus. But the church teaches that those are bad trees, those are 'bad books,' and that it is impossible for good fruit to come from those bad trees, and that any literature that is not sanctioned by the church is, well, spiritually dangerous. After all, one could easily be led astray by the subtle and seductive wiles of the devil. Authors and organizations outside the doors of the church are not to be trusted. And yet these young adults see secular institutions often doing more for the future of our world than the church is. They see the unfair, judgmental way the church has taught them to view their neighbors, and they know all is not right with this bubble-like, separatist view of humanity.

They've grown tired of the continual promotion of fear, guilt, and all the rules, and all the social and emotional manipulation, and all the quirky (outdated) '70s style social exclusiveness, and all the philosophical control and intimidation. They became tired of all the shepherds, and all the shepherding. They got tired of the "stand up, sit down, stand up, turn around, repeat after me, shake the hand of the person next to ya," musical chairs format. And they grew incessantly done with someone else trying to define, maintain, and control the way they feel about themselves on a regular, scheduled weekly basis, in a format that reeks of dependency, emotionalism, obligation, and intimidation, rather than freedom, liberty, individuality, expression, and inclusiveness. They see the church as a place to learn how to feel bad about themselves – so they can then get the full instructions on how to feel good about themselves again. There is something deeper, simpler, freer, and more all-inclusive about God, and about life itself that their parents' organized religion has failed to uncover. And somehow, they know it.

Young People Leaving the Church (Pastor's Bass Boat, and a Real, Live Giraffe!)

The youth of today asked the tough questions but got the same old answers. They left the church because of the never-expanding theology, not because there are no muffler-free, motocross races behind the building on Wednesday night. They left because they were told what to believe rather than why to believe it, not because the Sunday morning service doesn't start with an MTV-style slide show on a monster, house-sized HD screen with louder-than-usual 'rock' music. That might work for the 13-year-olds, but the young adults in their 30s can no longer be bought with loud, shiny things or by bringing zoo animals, motorcycles, and bass boats into the sanctuary.

I am very optimistic about the future. We have been thinking for years that what needs to happen is the current church being fixed, or *repaired*, or *reformed*. Those are noble thoughts, but what is actually happening right before our sleeping eyes is that the church is being completely replaced, and it is a good thing, because the current form of 'Christianity' is not at all what was supposed to happen in the first place. Jesus was never meant to become an obligation-based, guilt-based, paying God-based, Jesus-only religion. I do not believe it was ever supposed to happen.

Are 'People' Replacing Pastors?

Pastors are people too, but the times, they are a-changin'. The way we are forming our theology today is so much different than the last generation. Over the years, it never dawned on me: the church tradition of paying one man to tell us what God is saying or, what a certain passage in the Bible really means, is coming to a close. Although I do have a lot of respect for a person who dedicates their entire life helping others to better understand God, themselves, and the world we live in, shouldn't that be the continual, natural occupation of everyone?

Many humans have been led to believe they need another human that is smarter than them and somehow closer to God than them to lead them. Yes, people actually believe that. This has become a subconscious cultural norm that we have long-since accepted as true. And there is value in listening to spiritual devotees, but the inherited premise that shepherds and pastors and leaders of people's spiritual lives is a given necessity is just not true. The days of us getting in our cars, driving to a building to pay one man to give us "something from God", are coming to an end. Ironically, such a spiritually lazy cultural construction never took place in the first, second, or third centuries of the church that Christianity so often boasts of trying to follow.

So, why have we been paying one person to study and pray and meditate for us? Is it because they would then have more time than us 'forty hour per week' employees out here? Were they smarter than the rest of us? Was it because God had 'called' them and somehow gave them deeper insights into all things spiritual? Many preachers often point to the early 'church record' as the proper template for modern-day church structure. "And He gave some as apostles, and some as prophets, and some as evangelists, and some as pastors and teachers," etc. (Eph. 4:11, also 1 Cor. 12:28). But how does what some ancient Middle Eastern people did, or how they structured their get-togethers to talk about God, have anything to do with us here in the twenty-first century? We are not ancient Middle Eastern nomadic Palestinians. Why do preachers insist that ancient Middle Easterners are somehow the model that we must use in fellowship? Have you ever thought about that?

The Information Age

Now, with the Internet, and especially Facebook, we are able to get all those sermons for free, from (literally) dozens of spiritual writers, speakers, even pastors, and from many different sources, angles, and points of view. So driving to a building to listen to one person; what's the point? Social loyalty? Do we need a leader? Is it for the fellowship? Anyone can attest to the experienced-fact that two meaningful hours of "fellowship" with three or four people at a local park or family barbeque is a much more beneficial/quality experience than singing songs with 500 people in a big room. But are we (actually) ready to wake up to these facts and simple, observable truths? If it is for the fellowship or 'corporate worship,' then that seems like a good reason, but do we have to pay money for fellowship? It's nice to have a building I guess, you know, where we can all meet and have dinners and such.

Looking back over my own personal life in the church, if I am to be honest, I relied on pastors to do most of my seeking God, studying, and meditating for me. And I really do not think I am being too presumptuous when I say this is probably true for most churchgoing folks. After all, that is what we were paying the clergy for, right? And that whole *concept* or *traditional function* of a spiritual leader does create, promote, and even nurture a certain level of trusted dependency, does it not? Let's be honest. Of course it does. It also creates an expectancy of the pastor 'having something from God' to give us every Sunday morning. And there is value in this, and there always was; but was it the most optimum of possibilities concerning one's own spiritual growth and enlightenment? I think these are really good questions, don't you?

I don't think local churches with pastors are wrong; I just believe they are on their way out. What age group is the tithe money coming from right now? Where will they be thirty years from now? One doesn't need a master's degree in common sense to realize that many of the churches in town will eventually be converted into commercial office space. To many, this is a sad thing, but to others it is a positive, natural evolution of 'church' returning to its more original second-century form.

Giving financial support to voices that are helping us grow is a beautiful thing all about love and freedom and sharing. But it would appear to me that the role of pastors is indeed being replaced by people, and that the platform of accommodating spiritual enlightenment is changing very fast from professional, organized institutions to grass-roots brothers and sisters simply sharing from their hearts their own stories and experiences and revelations. People are becoming less afraid of somehow accidentally hearing some 'less than doctrinally correct' theology, understanding that even if they do, their heart will help show them along the way, and plus, now, more than ever before, they (literally) have a "cloud of witnesses" to help them.

Rather than being afraid of certain puzzle pieces, we are now talking openly about them and helping each other find out where they fit or don't fit. We don't need a referee, or someone to protect us from outside information. And if we can be honest with each other that is also a big part of the role pastors have often played. They have wanted to *protect* us like we are a bunch of otherwise wandering sheep that are mentally and spiritually incapable of processing conflicting information on our own.

More on Money

If all the church building & maintenance and clergy salary funds were spent on world hunger and the homeless, there would be no hungry humans on the face of the earth (with a billion dollars left over for other world-changing stuff). This is a well-established financial fact. Do we care? No, we most certainly do not. As a matter of fact, most church-going folks would NOT make that trade, nor do they like even being presented with the idea. The "church" then of course would be "reduced" to very small home group fellowship meetings and picnics and parishioners being forced to do their own truth-seeking, and neighbor-loving. Some folks think that would just be "too great a price to pay"... even though what I just described is in fact an accurate reflection of the early first, second, and third-century "church". An extremely revealing and well-researched book I would highly recommend on this subject is "Pagan Christianity" by Frank Viola and George Barna.

Here's the "worst" part of this...

If all of a sudden there were no church buildings, most of the money spent on that system would probably not go to feed the world's hungry and poor, but simply go back into the pockets of those who once attended those buildings. Why? Because, with no one to tell them what to do with their money, they would have to decide for themselves what to do with it. We could call this, um... "Returning to Real", or ... "Returning to honesty". You know... "Each one according to what they purpose in their heart to give..."

Grow Up, Saints

Years ago, I actually remember hearing a preacher in Florida saying that he would love to see the day when his congregation grew to the point of putting him out of business. Knowing the heart of that particular pastor, I think he was genuinely serious (and actually cared that much about people's spiritual growth). His dream is coming true, and on a much wider scale than he could ever have imagined. For decades, pastors have all often communicated between other fellow pastors one main concern: that their parishioners would make more concerted efforts to personally grow up spiritually. That is now actually happening. And although some pastors are happy to see it, others with ever-dwindling attendance charts are probably thinking, "Be careful what you wish for."

Change Is Inevitable, Growth Is Optional

I totally believe in the freedom for those who wish to attend a church. I am not against people who attend church, but simply pointing out how the current preacher, pulpit, stage, microphone, 'sit down, stand up,' 'be reverent in the house of the Lord' days are coming to a close in our generation. And again, that is not a bad thing.

I am not overlooking all the wonderful, charitable, and benevolent programs, benefits, and social luxuries of local gatherings of like-minded people. Many local churches reach out to the hurting and people in need and have been a place of healing for many. What I am speaking about here is the role of 'pastor' (in the realm of preaching and teaching theology). The long-held custom of having one person authoritatively telling us what to think is on its way out. And so is the fear-based 'art of protectionism' from any information or theological concepts that disagree with the denomination headquarters. When mainstream Christianity finally loses their hell doctrine and their dark, scary apocalyptic future, there will be nothing left but sharing and caring. When all fear is finally gone, love will rule quite naturally.

Church Attendance Is Dropping for a Reason

Although there are local churches that are growing in attendance, every Christian denomination in the country is deeply concerned about a nationwide trend of church attendance dropping significantly in this generation. Perhaps stopping it, or *fixing* it isn't as much the answer as is accepting it and embracing it as a natural culture change of a new age, and then really trying to understand what is going on, and how we are growing out of one mode and into another. 'People caring for people' is something we will never grow out of.

Seven

THE LATE PICKERS

It is not learning new things that the progressives are doing, but older things than the "old things" their grandparents were authoritatively taught. Much of the obsession of preserving inherited doctrines is not based on wisdom, but romance and loyalty.

About five years ago, my wife and I would often chance upon Dr. Wayne Dyer and his spiritual seminars on PBS (Public Broadcasting System). Having been thoroughly indoctrinated by the church, I was almost certain I could clearly see where Mr. Dyer was teaching several things that were in sharp contradiction with the scriptures. His messages were absolutely captivating, and although he was saying things that my head believed were wrong, my heart somehow knew these same things were right. If we had not first gotten the church's grossly flawed eschatology and doctrine of hell corrected, none of these more progressive spiritual writers would have taken up ten minutes of our time without being tossed into the garbage for being 'contradictory to the scriptures.' Once we had those exegetical problems fixed it became more than obvious that these New Thought authors were actually closer to the essence of the teachings of Jesus than the church was. "*Shocking!*" is an understatement!

Love Wins and *Raising Hell*

Along came Rob Bell with his book *Love Wins*, which was mostly just a collection of questions about hell and some other long-held doctrines many church leaders were quite upset about him even asking about. But what were they all of afraid of? I had to find out, so I bought the book. And what I found was nothing more than one man asking some of the tough questions that we all have secretly asked ourselves over the years. This book quickly led us to *Raising Hell* by Julie Ferwerda, which finally answered most of our unanswered questions about the church's doctrine of 'hell.' Rob and Julie's books finally gave us the permission to start asking the harder questions without feeling irreverent about it.

The Secret and *The Power*

Suddenly I realized that if it was okay to read stacks of Christian authored commentaries and novels that were full of opinion and theory, then it should also be okay to read positive literature not sanctioned by the church. A dear New Age friend of mine gave me a copy of Rhonda Byrne's *The Secret*, which led to my purchase of *The Power* by the same writer. The most shocking thing about these two Law of Attraction books is that they were, in essence, scientific explanations of many of the Biblical principles we had already been taught about sowing and reaping, and the workings of Spiritual Law, or as some preachers call it, the Law of Reciprocity. One could scribble scripture references in the margins of almost every page of her books! I was beginning to wonder if her scientific views were hopeful explanations of biblical principles or if the teachings in the Bible were actually hopeful explanations of science itself. A Christian friend of mine quickly accused Rhonda of stealing all her concepts from the Bible and then simply reformatting them into a New Age book just to make money. This certainly did not seem to describe the heart of the writer at all. In time, after reading dozens of unrelated New Thought Spirituality books, I found them all teaching the same principles. How could this be?

Inspiration

This led my wife and I to Dr. Wayne Dyer's book entitled, *Inspiration*. In very short order we had read his entire collection, and began devouring the works of people like Joshua Tongol, Jim Palmer, Rhonda Byrne, Eckhart Tolle, Deepak Chopra, Marianne Williamson, Michael A. Singer, Gregg Braden, Uell S. Anderson, Rumi, Osho, Louise Hay, Neville Goddard, Anita Moorjani, Lissa Rankin, Pam Grout, and too many others to list. We also began reading the teachings of Buddha, *A Course in Miracles*, and devotionally meditating on the 81 verses of the Tao. We continued to read the teachings of Jesus in our Bibles, but now with a whole new light. Ironically, what we found was that all these different writers sounded like they could have actually travelled with Jesus himself. Yet according to the church's prejudice, they were supposedly anti-Jesus.

Naming These Authors the "Late Pickers"

Many religious people have another name for them: The "wicked," as we have all heard them called. In reality, they are brothers and sisters, you know, the ones found doing the things of the law, when they don't even have or even know the law.

I have named all these authors that now seem more like old friends, the "Late Pickers", because they are a striking analogy of the late pickers found in the parable of the vineyard laborers in Matthew 20:1-16. Please take the time to thoughtfully read those verses. Would Christians of today respond in the same manner as the early pickers in this parable did? Unfortunately, I think many of them sadly would, and sadly do.

Here is the rationale: "Hold on just a minute! Why should those late pickers get the same pay as us? It's not right, and it's just not fair! I've been going to church my whole life, sometimes three times a week, living for the Lord, faithfully paying my tithes, studying the scriptures, sacrificing time away from my family to work at the church, living a life that is pleasing to God, and you're going to tell me that these 'never been churched,' candle burning, gem collecting New Age hippies are going to get the same eternal payment that I'm getting? If new, undiscovered truth is going to be uncovered in our generation, it is not going to come from all those secular New Thought authors before my pastor finds out first!"

If ever there was a Bible passage that has repeated itself throughout history, this is it. Here comes the twenty-first century late pickers and they're all talking about love, health, healing, freedom, power, and *worst of all* -- science. They are assigning names to God like Source Energy, and Divine Subconscious Mind, and even titles such as The Universe, or simply, Spiritual Law. Some of them are even brazen enough to call God the Great I AM. And they are actually producing a massive harvest! Countless millions of people all over the planet are becoming totally changed because of this new, vastly misunderstood revival of truth. If we look even deeper into it all, we find that the remarkably consistent fruit of this movement is making a broader, worldwide difference in the lives of people than we had first realized. What are we to do with these non-churchgoing spiritual gurus? "Compete with them!" shouts a man holding a Bible in his hand. And that is sadly just what many churches are doing.

Our Generation's Theological Reformation

> "Do not make what you currently know your boundaries. There is so much still for you to discover, and perhaps even the most important things." – Jim Palmer

Ferdinand Magellan discovering that the earth was round will not hold a candle to the theological reform that is about to take place over the next two decades. It is very encouraging to personally know so many people in my own social group who are not at all surprised at this declaration. But I am absolutely shocked at the number of people, namely Christians, who are completely unaware of what is just about to take place (in their own lifetimes). There is an historic theological shift taking place right now in this very generation that will undoubtedly prove to be the greatest theological reformation in history. Just look at what is going on with so many in the Grace Movement. Another exponentially growing phenomenon is the return of Universal Reconciliation. And the Preterist Movement is quickly becoming impossible for pastors to continue trying to sweep under the church carpet undetected, as if it has no exegetical integrity. And what are Christians doing reading Rob Bell and Jim Palmer books, or worse yet, the likes of Dr. Wayne Dyer, Gregg Braden, Deepak Chopra, or Rhonda Byrne? They are doing what their grandparents' era of theologians didn't have the stomach for: namely, connecting the awkward and uncomfortable dots of truth regardless if they start eating away at the shoreline of their predecessors' long held doctrines. When these brave revolutionaries are asked, "Why can't you just leave Christianity the way it is?" they simply answer, "Why are you afraid of the church's current concepts of God getting bigger?"

Is our current generation getting close to the end of finally figuring out all the messages and meanings of the Bible, or are we not just now (finally) nearing the very beginning of such things. That's a humbling thought, isn't it? The current theological reformation taking place all around us is a very welcomed sight for many, while at the same time, just a little scary for others. This reminds me of Jim Carrey in the movie *The Truman Show* when he lays his hand on the painted wall at the end of his 'known' world. People from every continent on our planet are right now finally uttering the words, "I had no idea! I had no idea!" More of them than you would think are from the same evangelical background as myself.

What if our unwillingness to listen to the New Thought authors and other spiritual sciences of today is actually keeping us from the deeper truths about God, ourselves, and the world we live in? Are all those writers and speakers really just a bunch of lost, wandering souls who go around rebelliously creating theological inventions simply because they 'don't want to be Christians'? Really? Can we fairly just lump them all together in one big stereotypical group of 'universe worshippers' all because we are not willing to consider the credibility and sound reasoning of their theology? Is that us?

Over the years I have heard people say that one cannot comprehend the Bible simply by reading it with an academic, critical mind. Perhaps the same is true for those who are not willing to open their hearts to inspired resources outside the church. Imagine if it were actually true that only ancient, Middle Eastern Jewish men were 'inspired by God' to write things on flat surfaces. Just sayin'.

FIELD OF GRASSHOPPERS

The Old Farmer and the Presidential Candidate

A Presidential candidate was trailing miserably in the polls in his last few weeks of campaigning. All the "qualified" people around him were giving him the best advice highest education and money can buy, but his numbers were not recovering. As his bus was passing through some no-name rural area of southern Idaho he spotted an old farmer on a tractor. After instructing the driver to pull over, he grabbed a small notebook, and going against the advice of his body guards, walked out into the humble field. From the bus window his advisory team members watched as he stood at the base of the large, muddy tractor wheel, asking questions, and taking notes (for almost an hour). The following day, with notebook in hand, he gave the speech that won him the Presidency. Go figure...

Don't be surprised when the answers to some of your deeper questions come from the most unsuspecting people and places. I have actually experienced having some of my life-long theological questions finally answered by people in the New Age camp (of all places), when I was absolutely certain that could never happen. As a matter of fact, I learned more about the very essence of the teachings of Jesus from people outside the church than I did from well-educated preachers and seminary professors. How is that even possible?

I once had a homeless fellow totally revolutionize my thoughts on loving your neighbor *as* yourself. He told me that I was "only fooling myself" to think such a thing is even possible until I was first able to truly *see* my neighbors as myself. I have never heard that sermon from a pulpit. And then, shockingly, I was continually and consistently shown (by example) how to unconditionally love and accept other people from an atheist co-worker named Jason. It took a young girl covered with tattoos and piercings, in very unrefined language peppered with passion-filled swearwords – to really drive home to me how many so-called "followers of Jesus" are actually following a politically-conservative brand of something they call "Christianity" (and that a simple study of Jesus' teachings reveal a much different philosophy than much of mainstream evangelical Christianity). I certainly didn't see that coming either! I finally got my eschatology corrected by a self-educated gal named Dotty who has been completely ostracized and branded as "out in left field" by her entire family (for being an honest-to-herself truth seeker, of all things). I finally got the church's long-held doctrine of hell and eternal punishment corrected by a guy who can't spell some of the most commonly-used words in the English language. In two short minutes from watching some guy on P.B.S. (Public Broadcasting System), I have gotten profound, concise answers to questions a hundred world-renown theologians could not answer for me OR for themselves.

I have learned great, world-changing things from millionaires and drunks, overly-educated, doctrinally-arrogant scholars, and people who never made it through the eighth grade. They all have had valuable contributions for my life. One of my greatest mentors in life, teaching me about being true to myself, was a life-long pastor named Clarence St. John. Amazing, life-altering truth often does come from the "qualified" places you think it should come from, and yet at other times it just waits patiently for us in the heart and mind of the waitress, the well-digger, or the service adviser at the car dealership.

PS: Ever wonder why some of the best food is found in little hole-in-the-wall joints off the beaten path, and being cooked by an old lady who uses no recipes?

And After All, We're Only Ordinary Men

> "They drew a line that shut me out, heretic, rebel, a thing to flout! But love and I had the wit to win. We drew a circle and brought them in." – Edwin Markham

I remember distinctively hearing a preacher once admonish his congregation to be more willing to allow others to speak wisdom into their lives. Unfortunately he was not referring to 'others' outside the doors of the church. When some of us leave Christianity, many churchgoers will no longer be able to consider us as brothers and sisters. However, we can and will continue to consider them as ours. We could "love the Christian but hate their doctrines," but that would make us into the very sad thing we no longer want to be. And continuing that division and separation, God only knows it's not what we would choose to do. When we finally (and truly) see our neighbor as ourselves, we can then and only then actually love them as ourselves. Our view towards others reflects our view of God: If we believe God accepts all, we accept all. If we believe God doesn't accept all, then we do the whole 'us vs. them,' fear-driven dance. How can we see God as unconditional love and the Great Terminator of eternal souls at the same time? We can't, and we know we can't.

From a Goat's Point of View

There is a social price you pay when your theology changes from Evangelical Christian to New Thought Progressive. Some of your religious friends and family will stop encouraging you and giving you a thumbs-up for anything you say and do, whether religious in nature or not, as if you have now somehow lost all philosophical value. They are afraid that if they encourage you on anything, you may mistakenly see it as an endorsement or acceptance of your conflicting philosophy. Or worse yet, one of their peers may see it as such. This religion-based fear (and lack of freedom) actually builds a wall between themselves and the very people they love and care about. They no longer want to truly know the loved ones who have moved away from their treasured doctrines; therefore, if we are to be honest, they now value religious doctrines over people. The results of this horrible religious dysfunction, are close friends and family members socially divorcing the very people they 'love.' Yes, it is insidious.

When Love is Allowed to Leave
(the difference between unity and uniformity)

If you think that much of modern day mainstream evangelical Christianity is not an exclusive, separatist-driven religion of fear and obligation, try this - leave it and start entertaining the more progressive theology of our time, start talking to people in the church you came from about your exciting and liberating new discoveries, then sit back and watch them talk behind your back, try to publicly discredit (and completely distance themselves from) anything you have to say – all in front of their peers of course, so they are "safe" from not being "led astray" by your scary, blasphemous "declarations of spooky darkness".

Then, a sort of ... "circling of the wagons" takes place. You, who were once celebrated and even promoted (when you believed the same as them), are now a threat and a danger. Anyone from "the group" who is seen encouraging you, or attributing any value to what you have to say, or celebrating your new-found happiness (in any way) could be easily mistaken for supporting your new philosophies... which could easily be mistaken (by members of the group) as endorsement. Better (and safer for the group) to just treat you as though you now have leprosy.

So... you are my "brother" or my "sister" as long as you continue to believe what I believe? Really? That's how that works? My heart tells me that there's something extremely wrong with that...

All too often the way in which the church deals with those who have left the faith is to leave the one and go after the ninety-nine who are still with them (which is the opposite of what Jesus taught). A friend recently told me... "The church is not bound together by love as much as they are by agreed-upon doctrine. Step outside of that circle and you'll know the true meaning of 'outside the circle'."

People who leave the church/or faith are often socially divorced with the same flippant attitude one has of shutting a screen door on the neighbor's cat (Even unfriending them on facebook to make any possible sight of them disappear). Such heartless behavior can be compared only to some 1969-style Mafia family banishing their own. According to what the church teaches, it would seem the instinctive thing to do would be an immediate attempt to contact those who have left, in a sincere Christ-like loving desire to understand the person, and then from that place of compassion and understanding attempt to correct them, or guide them back to 'the path', and gently restore them (2 Timothy 2: 25, 26).

What is often done instead is just the opposite. The exiting truth seeker frequently finds themselves on the harsh end of a warning campaign (Translation: gossip campaign), where they are branded and marginalized as "out in left field", or as "sadly lost", or even as "downright dangerous". And it gets worse... Any corrective theological information that 'backslidden' prodigal shares about what they used to believe compared to what they now believe - is to be seen as an angry, heartless, and blasphemous "attack" on those still in the church, Christianity, the Bible, and even on Jesus himself. It becomes more important to discredit the wayward traveler than trying to help them. They have become a philosophical danger to the collective, and are treated accordingly.

I am beginning to understand why Jesus wasn't all that popular in some religious circles. There's the 'talk', and then there's the 'walk'. All too often, they are two very different things.

A friend of mine, Kevin, from Greenville, Michigan, said this:

> "When we no longer agree on doctrine, the 'relationship' cannot be allowed to continue, and the one who 'strays' is now treated as if they are a danger to society. This behavior displays complete disdain for Christ and all He stands for. Love gives absolutely no thought to doctrine, or like-mindedness. Love just loves."

Vanessa, from South Africa, says this:

> "It's like you're not part of their circle anymore, you can talk about other stuff but it's as if they've made a pact not to talk about any religious talk with you and if you say anything in that line, it's brushed off quickly so a conversation about religion doesn't develop."

Martin, from Slovakia, had this to say:

> "My wife and I are living this religious nightmare right now, losing our friends. It is such nonsense, such dangerous, destructive, and sad religious nonsense."

Lisa, from Nashville:

> "I came from a large, extended family of staunch Pentecostals. The hurtful part of my story was learning through the grapevine of several family members -- aunts, uncles, cousins -- talking among themselves about me after I left the church, of how I was now 'out in left field,' along with warning other family members about me. They were concerned enough to talk about me behind my back, but not enough to contact me personally out

of Christ-like love or Christian care to help me get back on the right path. Not one of them. Could it be that they are afraid to approach me because of fear that they might learn something real from me? Or were they just never really the genuine people they always postured themselves to be? When I was in the church they 'loved' me. Now I seldom hear from any of them. I have privately forgiven them and moved on, because they really 'know not what they do' or how they treat people."

Another person, anonymous, as requested, still struggling from the rejection of Christian family members, had this to share from her heart:

"If only the Christians would let us live with them as neighbors ("Neighbors", where have I heard that word before?). I've done way more than my fair share of accommodating the religious people around me! I do my best to focus on what we have in common and remain graciously silent over things I strongly disagree with them on. They are the dogmatic ones who have to take issue with things we don't see the same way. They get offended, unfriend me on Facebook, and even in real life, and then wag their tongues about me to everyone who will listen. We can accept them but their refusal to accept us prevents relationship from surviving differences of doctrinal beliefs."

Bottom line: You cannot truly love your neighbors *as* yourself until you can honestly *see* them as yourself. If your inherited doctrines can all-of-a-sudden cause you to separate yourself and distance yourself from those you once enthusiastically embraced and claimed to "love", and then mentally decide that they no longer have any spiritual value to you, then your doctrines are sorely lacking, period. I'm sorry, but there is no gentle way of saying that.

My friend, Reine, says this:

It's very difficult for some people to get past the hurt, the not understanding when someone leaves their "faith", their "church"... it's because they just do not understand, and it causes them (weather they realize it or not), to question themselves and their own belief system... after all, the person who left, questioned it, and found different answers, so there must be more out there, right? It is scary to them! There IS something wrong with this picture when people divide themselves from those who don't agree anymore on their personal beliefs. But I believe that DEEP DOWN, it really DOESN'T matter to people, but that there's an uncomfortableness that they don't know how to respond to when they know things have changed. There are examples time and again of someone "in trouble", whether it be someone on the street, someone who has been misplaced due to tornado, fire, etc., or someone who is hurt in an accident of any kind.... people reach out immediately. They don't stop first to say "are you a Christian?" or "What are your Religious beliefs"? No, they reach out; they help one another because it's the right thing to do for your brother or your sister; a fellow human being, who is really, just like you. Ultimately, it does not matter, and I think more and more people are beginning to realize that, thank God.

Religion Fighting Truth (Can You Imagine That?)

Have you ever in your life rebuked truth in the name of Jesus, actually thinking you were coming against the lies of the devil? Could the church actually be fighting truth itself on many doctrinal issues and not even know it? Is that even possible?

I was (literally) afraid of truth itself. How silly is that? I couldn't bear to just sit and watch pieces of my treasured ideological concepts fall away like the thoughtless sandy banks of some no-name river. And if I am to be completely honest with you, that is what kept me so long from what I now so clearly see. Guess what? There's more, and like that childhood Sunday school song "Deep and Wide," it actually is deeper and wider than we once thought. Those books that we don't want to read actually are full of fundamentally important stuff that the church has completely missed, and they actually do hold important, indeed crucial, answers for humanity if we really hope to graduate to the next level of spiritual understanding.

For many, the protection and preservation of the institution called "Christianity," or more pointedly, the version we inherited from nineteenth-century hymnists and lofty Bible commentators, has, in many ways, actually become more important than truth itself.

The Patchwork Quilt

I am now learning, as a person 'coming out' of Christianity, that we didn't have a belief system; we had dozens of belief systems. They were all sown together into a large and comforting patchwork quilt. To start removing certain patches here and there throughout that quilt was much too awkward, embarrassing, and even too disheartening to consider.

The solution? Remain loyal to the entire quilt and just don't talk about the awkward, incorrect patches, because removing or exposing the incorrect patches (doctrines) would be too much work. There are just too many of them, and it would force us to have to (publicly) rethink the entire quilt itself. Keeping all those doctrines safely intact for the followers had become even more important than truth itself. Plus, the world was watching, and so we had to maintain the perception of theological confidence and exegetical superiority so they didn't see us sweating. Hence, making allowances for some untruths was, well, acceptable, just as long as the main message was correct and lives were being changed. That's like saying, "Dropping a thousand Bibles from an airplane might kill one small child from head trauma, but just think of all the others who will find God because of the many Bibles now in the village."

Serious fundamental-level theological reformation was not a necessity that we really had the gut stuff to even consider, let alone admit, as desperately needed. That's why just repainting that same old siding a different color, you know, remodeling the terminology or reformatting the communicative style (decade after decade after decade) continued to be business-as-usual.

Finally I had to ask myself, "How many doctrines have to be quietly readjusted or subtly reformatted with new terminology so the parishioners won't notice the leadership's prior authoritative certainties? How many subjects stealthily and conveniently need to disappear from the Sunday morning bulletin before everyone notices a pattern of a lack of social transparency? How many pieces of that old quilt have to be switched out with new, upgraded patches without telling the congregation when and why it was done? And when will some pastor have the courage to (actually) step up to the microphone and make that humble announcement?" Actually, I know that pastor. His name is Frank. He got fired.

Many Christians have been hopefully (and romantically) anticipating the whole 'everything that can be shaken will be shaken' thing. What they did not count on was that "everything" literally meant "everything" (which includes many of their own treasured doctrines).

The Circle

Seeking the answers that we are certain we've already found is called "a circle." Circles don't really go anywhere except around and around and around, but at least we know where we are going -- to the same place we've always been. It's like the words of that old familiar song by Pink Floyd: "We're just two lost souls swimming in a fish bowl, year after year. Running over the same old ground ... what have we found? The same old fears."

Complete, blind loyalty to our inherited religion is very much like a teenage boy who still cannot get over the fact that his ex-girlfriend isn't all of who he wanted her to be. So he continues to tell himself, "She is, she is, she is!"

I am finally okay with truth being what it actually is, even if that means that the New Agers and New Thought authors have discovered some vitally important things that the church has completely missed. I am finally okay with that if it is the truth. That is a liberation that was oh, so hard for me to finally come to grips with and surrender to. But at one point in my journey, I had to ask the question and make the decision, "Am I a truth seeker, or a religion keeper?"

That's Me in the Corner. That's Me in the Spotlight…

I finally surrendered to the truth. There is no invisible Harry Potter-like battle taking place in the sky over my head for my soul, nor over my house for the spiritual lives of my children. All there is, and ever was, are choices and their interactions with God's universe-wide, eternally fixed Operating System/Spiritual Law. Everything else I had been taught was either teachings of ancient Jewish mysticism, metaphors, or analogy-driven hopeful attempts by well-meaning ancient men. They not only wrote their own religions, but also then, with the power they (we) possess, through the Law of Attraction, began to (actually) manifest their futures to coincide with their concepts. Yes, I actually do believe that. They claimed that this 'God' made man in *His* own image, but it is now being revealed that just the opposite is what really happened.

Growing up in evangelical circles, I was taught of a magic tree, a magic snake, a magic 'original sin' that somehow magically affected the spiritual DNA of every human ever to be born, magical words and beliefs, a magical cosmic Jesus, magical rituals, and a magical blood sacrifice as a magical solution to all the above.

What I sincerely believe we are just about to discover as a civilization is that the universal language for interacting with 'God' is not a particular religion with its procedures or correctly spoken or believed protocols, but rather feelings, desire, hope, imagination, passion, dreams, intention, attitudes, thoughts, beliefs, expectations, and yes, faith. We will eventually find, I sincerely believe, that all the magic is not in special words, declarations, doctrines, nor in some 'separate from us' Being or Divine Personalities, but in us and in the process of simple interaction with Spiritual Law. So simple that it 'couldn't possibly be true.' What if it really is no more complicated than that?

I honestly believe that within the next two generations Christians will eventually discover that most of their inherited religion actually belongs to a regional area called Jerusalem in the first century, and that the globalization, westernization, and literalization of much of that story was never what that Middle Eastern saga was even about. They will eventually understand that although there is a lot of wisdom and spiritual principles in the Bible, it is largely 'someone else's ancient story,' based on someone else's ancient culture and religion. As far as Christianity goes, when they finally come to grips with the fact that there is no location called hell, and that a physical Jesus is never coming back here (never was), all their other 'us vs. them' doctrines will begin to crumble as well, and they will finally see their neighbors AS themselves. You may say I'm a dreamer, but I'm not the only one. There are millions of us now, and that number is growing daily.

Eight

FIELD OF GRASSHOPPERS

"While you were hanging yourself on someone else's words, dying to believe in what you heard, I was staring straight into the shining sun." – David Gilmour

My journey from reality to religion and then back to reality has brought me through so many different stages: awkwardness, confusion, indifference, shock, and even a temporary period of anger. I've traveled the path of arrogance and humility, outrage and dismay, revelation and loneliness. Like Icarus, I have faced truth square in the eye, knowing that whatever wasn't real would melt away like the wax that held his feathers together. When you're no longer afraid of what you might lose, or how embarrassing it might be to concede forty years of doctrinal 'certainty,' and are willing to follow truth regardless of where it might lead, you will most certainly find yourself in places you once swore you would never go.

We should never be afraid of truth, because truth will never do us wrong. Truth will always bring more peace, rest, childlike wonderment, and freedom. For the first time in my life, I can honestly say that I love God with my entire heart, and I really do (honestly) love all my neighbors as myself, for now I actually see them as myself (absolutely no separation).

When we see ourselves as having everything, giving our best without qualifying the recipients comes quite naturally. When we finally understand 'oneness,' we notice that there are no small, unimportant people. There is 'us.' Why wouldn't I want to heal myself, love myself, care for myself, encourage myself, feed myself, clothe myself, inspire and encourage myself, and empower myself? Until we truly see our neighbors as ourselves, we cannot truly love them 'as ourselves.' This has always been the case, and always will be the case. If we still have to try to love people, it is not a character development issue, but a simple lack of understanding. There are 10,000 writers writing about this right now because five years ago there were 1,000 writing about it. Try continuing this math for the next five years, and you will get a glimpse of the future.

'Christianity' is not the only answer, and believe it or not -- neither is 'Jesus.' Truth is the answer: truth from Jesus, truth from Buddha, truth from Lao Tzu, truth from Christianity, Hinduism, Islam, and Judaism, truth from ancient Eskimos, American Indians, Aborigines, truth from your mother, truth from a good book, and even truth in an overheard conversation at Starbucks. Finding and accepting truth is what sets us free, not some cosmic space traveler who is telepathically communing with us from somewhere 'out there.' It was never the intent of Jesus to become an exclusive, separatist, 'only one way to God' religion, but that people would awaken because of his teachings, just as this was the goal of many other great spiritual teachers. If you want Jesus to be a 'magic Person,' that is okay with me, but it is no longer okay for me to view him that way. If you insist on believing in eternal punishment from some psycho 'God,' who sets up a system, where people 'send themselves' to hell, I respect your choice, but my new view of God just won't allow me to believe in such insane, science fiction-like mythological darkness about my Creator anymore. That's just crazy, and I believe our hearts have always known it.

Running Down a Dream

> "The kingdom of heaven is like a treasure hidden in the field, which a man found and hid again, and from the joy over it he goes and sells all that he has and buys that field" (Matthew 13:44).

Most of my life I have lived under the psychological pressure that I was either making God happy or sad. I can honestly now say that I do not believe that anymore. Nor do I any longer live with the constant mindset that it is somehow my life's job to make God happy. How unreasonable and arrogant is that? I no longer believe that when I make poor choices or live at a lower vibrational level that I have somehow socially wounded the Creator of the universe, and that the only way to once again be restored into 'right standing' is to obtain absolution for my crime (sin) from that ever-watchful eye in the sky. What an enormous burden for a person to be talked into bearing throughout their entire life! I didn't get this fixed by doing away with God, but by finally understanding the true, beautiful character of God.

Over the Last Couple of Years I Have Lost So Much

At the top of that list, I lost all my striving, and I lost all my fear. I lost all my low, doctrine-based thoughts about myself, and I even lost all my lostness.

Why are some people continually attempting to put me back under their doctrinal fears? It is all based on stuff 'you had better realize' and 'you had better understand' and 'you had better believe' and 'you had better have all your ducks in a row.' Some may say, "Christianity is not a religion, but a relationship," and that may be true for some, but when they add the words "or else," they betray and contradict their own romantic declaration. They have indeed mixed the beautiful with the ugly without even knowing it. I don't blame them, or their teachers, but their teachers' teachers.

"I Must Warn You of the Danger"

> "Birds born in a cage think flying is an illness." – Alejandro Jodorowski

Have you ever noticed that many fundamentalist Christian authors continually use the words "We must…", and "We need to…", or "We've got to…", or "We ought to ...", or "We had better..."? Sounds like someone who is in fear of losing something. What are they about to lose that has them so ... 'concerned'? It is like someone saying, "Hey man, if I have to be afraid, then so do you!" Whenever I hear phrases like "we must be careful" or "slippery slope" or "warning" or "in danger of" or "we must rightly divide the Word" or "guard yourself from" or "I'd be very leery of..." or "we should be very concerned about," having to do with any theological conversation, I see fear and insecurity, not wisdom (as such people actually believe they are exhorting). I see protectionism of a fear-based theology wherein they want to keep people where THEY are rather than allowing them to obtain more freedom 'than they should.' This wasn't as clear to me five years ago as it is now. Freedom and Love allow you to see things that you can't believe you couldn't see before.

No More Fear

Someone just asked me to consider making sure I've got my theological i's dotted and t's crossed *just in case* the church's dark and spooky doctrines of the afterlife are true; that way I've *got all my bases covered*. In other words, just in case God *is* a maniacal twisted freak of nature who *does* systematically terminate billions of souls that live on this planet for not loving Him correctly according to ancient Middle Eastern written procedures and protocols, I would be covered and rendered safe from Him. My answer? No thanks for such a horrifying version of God. I have been very happy ever since I walked calmly away from such dark insanity. If no longer believing that God is the Master Terminator of billions of souls places me in *dangerous waters*, then I'm going swimming. I'm sorry, but the Creator of the universe does not kill humans. It is just not true, and it never was true.

No More Striving

No more begging and pleading some external 'up there somewhere in the sky' God to please notice me 'down here below' and please fix my problems, and please give me strength to get through the day, and please forgive me, and please give me guidance, and please give me favor, and please make me a better Christian, and please open the doors, and please help me to please You more and to be a better servant, and please, please, please, please, please. We have been told that we are the salt of the earth, and the light of the world, and that God's love is in us, and yet we drop to our knees in seemingly endless pleading: "Oh Lord, please come down and be our salt and our light, and love people through us, and let us see the hurting through Your eyes!" But if I can't already see the hurting, then I'm either talking to the wrong God, or I have yet to experience Him in the first place.

Lowly Serfs

We were never meant to see ourselves as lowly serfs down in a humble valley working for some King in a distant castle. That depiction of lowly, obedient servant-hood, I am completely convinced, is something that is man-made and not at all the reality of who and what we are, or how our relationship with God was ever intended to look or feel. On one of my Facebook posts about realizing how beautiful we all truly are, a well-meaning Christian lady commented with these words: "Our mission in life is to be who God created us to be to serve *Him*. This world is not our true home." To me, this was someone's response designed to 'guard against' any of my readers who might pridefully get the idea that they are full of *light* and *beauty* and *value* to their fellow man.

I also once defined "freedom" as indebtedness and lowly, unworthy servant-hood. I also once daily prayed, "God please use me!" viewing myself as no more valuable than God's humble, little, otherwise worthless puppet, or 'vessel.' I also once wrongfully extracted my sense of value and self-esteem, or if I was 'in God's will,' on whether or not He was 'using me.' I also once thought it so noble to replace Moses with Jesus. That was me too, and not so long ago. I also once pleaded for God to give me *His* eyes and *His* heart in order to see the hurting, rather than realizing that I already see them with my own eyes. I don't need to learn *how to love*, or how to give, or how to reach out to others in need, or how to forgive. I do not need a teacher for those natural things. I do not need a pastor to teach me how to be a good husband, father, or son. I don't need to 'agonize in prayer' in order to obtain the heart of God. I was born with that heart. I was born in 'right standing with God,' and so were you. Yes, you were!

No more needing to start or end every conversation with the words "The Lord," and no more needing to 'give the glory to God,' as if failing to do so is somehow going to affect my spirituality or affect my humility. In my not-so-distant evangelical past, it seemed to me that we were often more concerned about the dangers of shining than not shining. And I don't need someone to tell me the correct way to 'shine,' or the correct way to think about shining. We were constantly making sure that we were staying humble at any cost. I have tried to imagine me giving the sun more brightness. That's how much sense "giving God the glory" makes to me now. I think for many people, "Giving God the glory" simply means "Be careful not to take any credit for your own life's positive outcomes, lest you become prideful."

One of the greatest paradoxes of living on this big, blue, atmosphere protected, ecological paradise is that we spend the first 75 percent of our time here wishing and hoping for something better, and the last 25 percent accepting that this is the 'something better.' I can't speak for my readers, but I am changing these numbers for my descendants. What on earth were we thinking?

No More Blood, Sweat, and Tears

No more 'praying through' or believing that any amount of moaning and groaning or falling on my face before God is going to somehow get God's attention any more than lighting a thousand candles will. Penance does not move, or nudge, or awaken some Guy in the Sky. I don't care what anyone says about it, what ancient verses they quote to support it, or what some church father accomplished by wearing out his knees. I'm done trying to pay an 'out there somewhere' God who in reality expects no such thing, and responds to no such thing. Earnest and sincere acts of devotion may change us, but not God. How on earth did we inherit such a small, burdensome concept of the Creator of the universe? I love what the fourteenth-century poet Hafiz said, "Even after all this time the sun never says to the earth, 'You owe Me'. Just think of what a love like that can do! It lights up the whole world." I owe God nothing, and yet God provides everything.

No More Measuring

No more comparing myself to others, or allowing preachers to intimidate me into measuring my Christian growth status. I cannot tell you how many "How well or poorly are you doing as a Christian?" sermons I have heard over the years. I now realize that it was all sold under the auspices of 'challenging the saints,' but in reality (whether intentional or not) it was an unhealthy promotion of guilt of never quite being enough. "How strong are you in the Lord? How much time are you spending in prayer and Bible study? What are you devoting your time to? Are you a good husband, wife, father, mother, daughter, son, or child of God? Are you mentoring your children in the ways of the Lord? Are you speaking boldly about God to the lost? Are you winning souls?" In a nutshell, "I owe, I owe, so off to church I go."

A very valued friend, who retired after a lifetime of ministry as a pastor, shared this as a New Year's resolution: "I resolve this year to leave behind the stress and worry of religion. For most of my life, in one way or another, religion has been something that has ruled me, made me fearful, made me feel inadequate, made me feel the need to seek God, find Him, do what He wanted, try harder, be better, repent of my short-comings, and live in a fog of conditional love. No more. This year, I am determined to just live, just love, just enjoy, and just be. No strings. No conditions. No stress. No worry. Happy New Year!"

No More Guilt and Shame!

No more feeling like I'm not enough just the way I am. No more doubting. No more wondering. No more wishing, hoping, or praying for heavenly confirmation of my worth or significance. And please, no more Bible-based teachings about significance just to make sure I'm basing my significance on the correct doctrinal teaching.

Just a few months ago, someone was telling me how bad they felt because they hadn't read their Bible or prayed for an entire week. I simply replied, "Really? You're going to do that to yourself?" This person was relieved when I explained how it is scientifically impossible for us not to be 'continually in prayer.' Every thought and feeling is, in fact, a prayer. Just a few days later, a woman, after attending a church service that (basically) asked people to measure their own benevolence, was telling me how she felt bad and unspiritual, like she was (her words) "letting God down" that she wasn't doing more to reach out to the downtrodden. I can't even express just how good it feels to be completely free from such incorrect, guilt-driven brainwashing!

No More Low Self-Esteem

My heart knows that I am not worthless, ugly, and pathetic without Jesus. Somewhere down deep inside me I have always known that I was not born a rebellious sinner in need of absolution for being a human.

No more "I'm nothing without you, oh God" declarations of unhealthily dependent, self-abasing, sackcloth-and-ashes style of psychological self-abuse.

No more sorrowful lamenting that I live on planet earth instead of somewhere in an outer space "heaven" with Jesus, you know, "face-to-face."

No more looking at uncomfortable or painful life experiences as God trying to teach me something, nor as some movie-worthy, paranormal-like spiritual attack by the evil one trying to steal my joy. Nonsense! I am finally taking full responsibility for myself, for my own sowing and reaping.

No more mentally transferring blame on an invisible monster that lives out in the woods behind my house, or just below the earth, for my own lack of personal growth, insecurities, hang ups, or addictions. And no more completely disregarding my own accomplishments as things that "God is doing in my life," to somehow stay humble as the dependent, wayward prone little piggy that I am.

No more basing my self-esteem on spiritual experiences that I interpret as the Creator of the universe personally 'working things out' behind the scenes in my personal life, but rather that I have been not only making good choices and thinking good, optimistic thoughts, but continually obtaining a keener comprehension of just how the universe actually works. Yes, it is that simple.

My Yoke is Easy

The reason that 'natural as the rain,' 'easy as an ocean breeze,' 'gentle as a slow moving river,' 'relaxing as a tropical vacation' freedom has often felt more like a faith-based declaration than an 'honest to myself' daily reality is because that is exactly what it has been for me for most of my life – a faith-based declaration. When I finally located the reason for that dilemma, I also finally found the freedom. For me, it had to do with a lot of religion-based fear, devotion-based guilt, inherited feelings of 'romantic' indebtedness, unworthy servant-hood-based obligation, and doctrine-based illusions of exclusive separation from other members of our planet.

Oh, But I Have Gained So Much

Knowledge, Freedom, Power, Innocence, and a really nice field -- the field of flying grasshoppers I left at age six -- childlike innocence and explorative, inquisitive awe.

I Love My Life!

I would actually go so far as to say I am 'in love' with life! I love everything that is living and I love everything that is dying. I love the all-atom governing Divine Intelligence that brought all this together, including an incomprehensibly beautiful, perfectly maintained universe-wide, Operating System that governs the interactions of every single thought throughout the entire universe! My adoration and childlike awe of this Energy, this Source, this 'God' (as we call it) is so much more to me than just mere appreciation for nature; it is in fact a very romantic and personal love affair that I cannot even begin to describe with human words. "Adventurous" is an understatement of what our life and marriage has become over the last two years!

I love what Dr. Wayne Dyer says, "I am realistic. I expect miracles." Once we started really learning how the universe works, the fun began… The connectedness that we have with this all-encompassing 'One' is a '*One*-ness' that is simply indefinable! It is, well, glorious. There simply is no reason to live in separation from this, either in mind or in doctrine, for in reality, it is just not scientifically possible.

All Fear is Gone

When all fear is gone, the only things left are joy, peace, personal power, amazing possibilities, an almost indescribable freedom, and new excitement for life every single morning! Truth is funny like that. I have finally obtained what preachers have taught so romantically about for years. A hundred men on a hundred horses could not take it away from me, or put me back under the religious apprehension of the possibility of not having all my doctrinal t's crossed and i's dotted. Like I said, I'm returning to innocence. Don't try to stop me.

Closing Thoughts

I started this book by talking about how there is something *natural* about God, and indeed life itself. Throughout the book I continually implied that there is a gap between the world that religion has painted for us and the real world that we actually live and die in. I have talked about viewing God as a Zeus-like Being and have also used the analogy of a Santa Claus-like character in the sky to describe the ways in which we have been taught to mentally formulate not only our picture of God, but also our relationship with God. I've talked about how ancient men have written God's part in the play, using human attributes and characteristics. I have also showcased in a somewhat artful style how, even with our current knowledge of the size of the universe, how we have been taught to remain within this very small judicial 'pleasing God' concept of an up-there-somewhere Entity Who selectively dispenses provision according to our behavior 'down here below.' We have looked into fifty years of the church's embarrassing past. We have revisited and thoroughly analyzed the Bible's version of eschatology and the 'hell' doctrine. We have stepped back and taken a realistic outside view at what some of our inherited beliefs really look like when placed up next to reality. I have shown my readers how a great deal of my personal journey has been about finally obtaining the freedom to think for myself, fearlessly using my God-given logic, intuition, and deductive reasoning, rather than simply continuing to remain blindly loyal to things my heart has always questioned.

I am now thoroughly convinced that we can discover a more accurate understanding of God, ourselves, and the universe by sitting on a bench near a calm lake, than we can in a library full of dusty old books on theology.

Maybe the Moody Blues were right all along:

"We are one. We're all the same. And life is just a simple game."

As You Walk Away

So what has this book been about? Was it about some poor, wounded Christian who got his feelings hurt at some local church and then just flippantly decided to become an enemy of Christianity? Is that what you are walking away with? Or is your heart seeing a different scenario that you can actually relate to on many levels? The subtitle of the book says that it is "One man's story," but it is also the story for many others. Like me, they are finally opening their eyes to a new generation's newly-revealed truths, and returning to that childlike state of complete, easy-as-an-ocean-breeze freedom, innocence, and awestruck wonder. It is not a journey without bumps and potholes, because of the unlearning road we have had to travel, but it is a true story, with a wonderful ending.

I hope my honest journey has given you the permission to start asking some of your own questions. One thing is so real for both Liz and I -- we love God more completely, and sincerely, and honestly now than at any other time period in our lives; and loving our neighbors as ourselves is finally something we no longer have to try to do, or try to do more, or try to do more sincerely. Until we truly saw our neighbors as ourselves, we did have to apply effort in something that was never supposed to need effort.

Our life now is all about the possibilities of gain, rather than the fears of loss or worrying about pleasing God. When you finally realize that you are in charge of your own life's potentials, making the right choices becomes a thing of adventure and exploration, rather than some strange sort of judicial-based, devotional obedience as an earth prisoner – waiting and hoping to be noticed, forgiven, empowered, and rendered acceptable by someone else's concept of a sky King. I know that sounds ... irreverent, but I really want you to think about what I just said.

If the end result is being absolutely in love with God, your Source with a heart that is perpetually full of gratitude, and honestly loving your neighbor as yourself, you may just be okay. But could it actually be that simple? Or is there more required? Upon finally finding real freedom and inner peace, I looked around, and no doctrine of any kind could be found. At first I thought it a bit odd. But then my heart said, "Yeah... that's what I kind of figured all along." It's like sitting at the end of an old wooden dock, and a wise man points and says, "Consider the water bug." What I had been looking for my entire life, ironically, was simply to be a six-year-old again. How could I not have seen that coming? "You must be changed back into little children." – Jesus

Becoming six again,
Your friend, Ken

"And in the end, the love you take is equal to the love you make."
–The Beatles

Note to reader:

Please think of one person you know who you'd like to share this book with, so they can see what you have seen here. Then direct them to the web address below...

facebook.com/fieldofgrasshoppers

Made in the USA
Lexington, KY
16 April 2014